LOVE WRITING

LOVE WRITING

A GUIDE TO WRITING AND GETTING YOUR ROMANCE NOVEL PUBLISHED (WITHOUT LOSING YOUR PERSPECTIVE, PASSION OR SANITY)

BY

VIRNA DEPAUL

WITH

TAWNY WEBER

Printed in the United States of America

TABLE OF CONTENTS

PART II: SEEING HOW IT'S DONE

APPENDIX

FIRST THINGS FIRST[1]: CALLING ALL WRITERS

So you want to write a novel? Maybe you've started one and just need a little push to finish it. Or maybe you've written one and want to write a second, third, or fourth? That's awesome! Whether you're just beginning to write or you have a few manuscripts under your belt, we hope this book helps you get a little closer to attaining your writing goals.

Writing is both a challenge and a joy. Being a successful writer starts with three things: 1) knowing yourself and what you really want out of your writing; 2) being willing to devote the time, money and effort necessary to achieve your goals; and 3) knowing what challenges you will face if one of your goals is to be or stay published.

If you're a less seasoned writer, this book sheds light on what are some of the most important writing concepts, but in one streamlined method, which includes various worksheets to help you in the writing of your story. In addition, it describes the hazards of pursuing publication while providing inspiration and guidance to overcome them. Finally, even if you're an experienced writer, we hope this book reminds you why you started writing in the first place and provides you with a new way of approaching your writing goals, as well as your story.

---

[1]   Just for fun, many of our headings begin with the titles from some of our favorite books! Using the titles in no way indicates the individual authors know us or endorse this book. The same is true when we quote or refer to a particular author. *First Things First* by Barbara Delinsky

TO TRUST A STRANGER[2]:
OR, IF YOU'D RATHER NOT, A LITTLE ABOUT US

ABOUT VIRNA

Virna DePaul was an English Lit major who practiced law as a criminal prosecutor for over ten years. She began writing in September of 2006 and by January had a top-notch agent and editorial interest from a New York publishing house. Despite that grand beginning, it took her a little over three years to make her first sale. When she did, she sold the first two books in a paranormal series to Berkley Publishing (Penguin Group). The first book, *Chosen By Blood*, comes out in May 2011. She also sold to Harlequin's romantic suspense line.

ABOUT TAWNY

Tawny Weber is usually found dreaming up stories in her California home, surrounded by dogs, cats and kids. When she's not writing hot, spicy stories for Harlequin Blaze, she's shopping for the perfect pair of boots or drooling over Johnny Depp pictures (when her husband isn't looking, of course). A lifelong romance reader, it took a push from her husband for her to try her hand at writing. She started in 2002, joining Romance Writers of America and going on to final multiple times in RWA's Golden Heart contest, as well as serving on a variety of chapter boards and offices. After winning the Harlequin Blaze Challenge, she sold her first book, *Double Dare* in 2006. In September 2010, her tenth Blaze, *Riding The Waves*, hits the bookshelves.

---

[2]   *To Trust A Stranger* by Karen Robards

LONG TIME COMING[3]:
WHY VIRNA WANTED TO WRITE THIS BOOK

I was an English major in college and primarily studied classic novels by authors who'd already passed away. I think this is why, on some level, I'd always felt that writers were above ordinary people. They were special. Geniuses. Plus, they had time and money to isolate themselves from the drudgeries and distractions of reality. Think: Italian villa and Colin Firth in *Love Actually*.

Nonetheless, I'd read romance novels for years and repeatedly had the urge to write one. Unfortunately, it seemed like an insurmountable task to learn all the "rules" involved. Eventually, I had three children and I was sure the dream was over before it had even started. I had a full-time job. Responsibilities. I was just an ordinary person. Sure I had an English degree, but I hadn't focused on creative writing. In fact, it had always scared me. Who was I to think I could write a novel?

So, my life led me in other directions....Before I began writing full time, I spent over a decade practicing law as a Deputy Attorney General for the Appeals, Writs and Trials Division of the California Department of Justice. In other words, I was an attorney. Unfortunately, when I told people what I did for a living, it was always with a hint of embarrassment. I don't think being an attorney is anything to be ashamed of (yes, you heard me right), but identifying myself as one never felt right, either. You see, although I was proud of the work I did, I knew early in my career that being an attorney was not my passion or purpose in life. Every time I said the words out loud, I felt like a fraud.

---

[3] *Long Time Coming* by Sandra Brown

Today, when someone asks me what I do for a living, I proudly say, "I'm a writer."

How cool is that?

Getting published didn't make me a writer. I was a writer before I left my law job and before I sold. I immersed myself in the writing community, joining five local writing chapters, attending conferences, and, more importantly, completing one full manuscript after another. I discovered what I loved almost as much as writing itself—my fellow writers, as well as the excitement of honing my craft.

Even so, it wasn't until I attended several romance writing conferences and close to 40 Romance Writers of America ("RWA") chapter meetings, and completed my third romantic suspense manuscript that I realized most of the craft I'd learned in bits and pieces could be combined into a streamlined process. In addition, in the three years it took me to sell, I often wished I'd been better prepared for (or at least warned about) the difficulties I would face.

One of the people who helped me on my writing journey was Tawny Weber. Tawny and I met through our local writing chapter but our friendship deepened when her daughter and my son became play date pals. While they talked Pokemon, we often talked writing. I learned we had many shared experiences, similar ambitions, and, most of all, a desire to give back by sharing what we've learned from so many other talented people over the years. Since we write very differently and have different perspectives, I asked Tawny if she wanted to collaborate on this book with me. To my great fortune (and yours!), she did.

Depending where you are in your writing journey, some portions of this book may be more helpful than others. Skip around. Pick and choose. Take what works for you and set aside the rest.

Living an authentic life complete with purpose and passion is the key to happiness, but only if you maintain balance and continue to have fun. As J.A. Konrath explains in his book, *The*

Newbie's Guide To Publishing, the Theme of his novels matches his philosophy in life: "Try the best you can, because trying is all you can do. But if you try too hard, life isn't worth living at all."

I try to live my life this way. Sometime I fail, but I keep trying. I hope that in some small way, this book and our stories encourage you to go after your dreams and live the life you want.

HOW TO USE THIS BOOK (AND WHY IT'S STRUCTURED THE WAY IT IS)

This book is divided into four parts. We start with the good news first—the top ten things a romance writer can do to write a good book. This includes breaking down a detailed method for plotting your book and various worksheets that can help you with writing your story. We start with this section because, in the end, writing a good book is what it's all about.

Part II deconstructs a published romantic suspense book, *You Only Love Twice*, by Lori Wilde. (Don't worry, there aren't any serial killers involved. Lori Wilde writes compelling suspense with a fun, sexy edge.) Part II focuses on how Wilde took advantage of the principles highlighted in Part I.

In Part III, we discuss some things you might want to know if you're pursuing publication. We do this by telling you (first generally, and then in more detail if you're curious) about our writing journeys and some of what we've learned so far. Like most writers, our journeys were full of challenges and disappointments, but because we persevered, we eventually achieved that first sale and additional success.

Finally, Part IV provides tips and worksheets to make the writing process easier. It also touches on miscellaneous information, defines terms, and lists additional resources to explore.

You May Be A Romance Writer If....

- People often ask when you're going to write a "real" book.
- You know what a "crit" is. You've probably bought one at one time or another at a fundraising auction.
- You stay up all night because you have to see how a story finishes.
- You think of yourself as a "plotter," "pantzer," or something in between.
- You're never without your "WIP."
- You occasionally exclaim, "Why didn't I think of that?!"
- You know how to print multiple pages on one sheet of paper.
- You're horrified by the thought of your father or your children reading your book.
- Working and gaining weight are often inextricably related.
- You walk around muttering, "the same but different."

CHAPTER 1

DOES SHE DARE?[4]:
MORE TO THE POINT, SHOULD YOU?

Do you really want to write a novel? If so, why? Whether your goal is to get published or not, writing a book requires a lot of skill, as well as dedication, courage, and perseverance. Consider the following:

REASONS TO WRITE A ROMANCE NOVEL
- You love to read them.
- You love to write.
- You've often thought about writing one.
- You have stories in your head to tell.
- You often mentally rewrite the endings (or beginnings or middles) of books as you read.
- You have a message to share.
- You want to entertain others and are willing to work hard to do it.

REASONS TO RECONSIDER:
- You think it'll be easy.
- You have no love for writing.
- You need to make money.

---

[4] *Does She Dare* by Tawny Weber

- You want to be published right away.

- You think writers are cool (which is true, but you don't have to write a book to hang out with them).

- You'll be devastated or judge yourself if you don't sell.

In choosing to write, you've set an amazing goal for yourself, but please don't ever think it's an easy one. Writing a complete novel, even a short one, is a lot of work. Furthermore, if your goal is publication, the journey towards publication can often be brutal.

However, if you're going to write, and if you're going to thrive mentally and physically as a writer, you need to accept the process for what it is. It's a bit like that Kate Perry song--you know, it's up and down, black and white, joy and grief, and every possible emotion in between. Reading this book and talking to other writers is a great way to learn what it's like. Once you know, don't be intimidated into quitting (or never starting). Be glad you know what you're facing. Train. Gather tools. Even take a break once in awhile. Make a realistic plan to achieve what you want and don't be blindsided when you encounter a few obstacles along the way.

As Tawny often says, "pull up your big girl panties" and get the job done. (If you're male, you get the drift—and thank you for joining us.) Remember, however, that for all the difficulties you'll encounter, you are not alone. Plus, for all the "bad" news, there's plenty of good. If you can keep perspective about the low points and the business side of publishing (most often they are the same thing), writing can be a joyful experience. You can meet wonderful, creative people, increase your skills and versatility, and write a book you would love to read. Moreover, getting published *is* possible so long as you don't give up.

Always, your primary task is to sit down and write. It gets trickier from there. You need to write a good book. You want to enjoy writing, of course. In the end, you want to consistently do both. Your patience will likely be tested the longer you continue to write, but, at the same time, your skill should constantly be growing. Hopefully, so will your passion and your confidence.

Write. Love writing. Love your writing life. Do all three and you're that much closer to writing a better book and selling it!

You May Be A Romance Writer If...

- You buy (maybe even use) a lot of sticky notes and highlighters.
- You send out query letters. A lot of query letters.
- You'd be willing to pay someone to publish your book (because you know if people could only read it they'd love you).
- You volunteer to judge others and then alternately feel great or horrified about your own writing.
- You write when others are sleeping.
- Your office is a Starbucks.
- The Internet History file on your computer would horrify your neighbors.
- You scour magazines for pictures of your "ideal" man, pin them to your bulletin board, and don't even feel guilty when your husband sees them.
- You find yourself wondering how you can make a "zombie" story sexy.
- You believe that rather than misleading young girls about what they can have, you are empowering them to demand what they deserve.

PART I:

DOING THE WORK TO WRITE

AND GET PUBLISHED

CHAPTER 2
A TREASURE WORTH SEEKING[5]:
WRITING THE BEST BOOK YOU CAN

Writing is truly our passion. However, as we will stress throughout this book, trying to get published can be brutal. We have suffered amazing highs and amazing lows, and one thing that has been able to keep us going is the knowledge that writing is both art *and* craft. Writers can explore different methods and different structures for writing. We can change genre, voice, and even the name we write under. We can focus on concrete ways to write better when our "best so far" turns out to be "not quite good enough."

In Part I of this book, we describe a 10-Step method that sheds light on important craft concepts (Theme, Story Question, Character, Conflict, Plot, Raised Stakes, Three Act Structure, Turning Points, Scene/Sequel & Resolution), but also actively leads you through the process of brainstorming, developing, outlining, and submitting your story.

---

[5] *A Treasure Worth Seeking* by Sandra Brown

BEST KEPT SECRETS[6]: TEN THINGS YOU CAN DO TO SUCCEED AT WRITING

(PREVIEW OF STEPS)

- STEP 1:   SET REALISTIC GOALS
- STEP 2:   READ, EXPERIMENT AND FAMILIARIZE YOURSELF WITH THE "10 FOR 10"
- STEP 3:   BRAINSTORM CHARACTER, BACK STORY AND PLOT POINTS
- STEP 4:   CONFIRM YOUR STORY FITS THE SUBGENRE/LINE YOU'RE TARGETING
- STEP 5:   EXPAND UPON YOUR STORY'S THEME; BRAINSTORM MOTIF AND SYMBOLISM
- STEP 6:   CREATE A LOG LINE, A STORY PREMISE, AND HIGH CONCEPT PITCH IF POSSIBLE
- STEP 7:   BRAINSTORM SCENES
- STEP 8:   WRITE A SYNOPSIS
- STEP 9:   WRITE AND REVISE
- STEP 10: SUBMIT, SURVIVE & START AGAIN

---

[6] *Best Kept Secrets* by Sandra Brown

CHAPTER 3
STRIKING DISTANCE[7]:
TAKE THE FIRST STEP THAT WILL
GET YOU THE FARTHEST

STEP 1: SET REALISTIC GOALS
"A Goal Is A Dream With A Deadline." --Napoleon Hill

Chances are if you're reading this book, you have a dream. A dream to write a novel. Maybe to get that novel published. One of the best ways to make your dreams come true is to set goals. We all know what goals are, right? They're things we want. Things we're striving for. Things we're willing to work for, not just desire. Here are some tips for setting and achieving your goals.

MAKE IT BLACK AND WHITE
"Vague Goals Produce Vague Results." --Jack Canfield

What, exactly, is a vague goal? One that doesn't clearly define the results you want. To write a novel is a great goal, but it's not specific enough. What kind of novel? How long? Do you want anyone to read it? What readers are you targeting?

In the same vein, to sell a book is another great goal, but again, it's not specific enough. This goal covers everything from self-

---

[7] *Striking Distance* by Debra Webb

publishing a "how-to" on building a steam engine, to selling a "book here and a book there" to different publishing houses in a variety of sub-genres.

So be specific. Specific but flexible.

You don't want to cheat yourself out of a goal. For instance, what if you start writing one genre and find you hate it? Or what if you target one publishing line, only to find the line closes? Being specific about your goal, but being able to adjust your goal in the face of obstacles, will increase your chances of accomplishing it.

A fun tool to help you narrow down your goal is to try and picture it. If you're a visual person, close your eyes and imagine the goal. See it in your mind as if it's happened already. For instance, see yourself in the bookstore watching people buy your book off the shelf. See yourself winning major writing awards or your name on the *New York Times Best Seller* list. Whatever your goal is, see it in your mind. If you're not visual, imagine how it will feel. Bring in the emotions and excitement you'll experience when it happens.

Once you've narrowed down your goal, honed it, and made sure this is exactly what you want, the best thing to do is write it down. Writing down your goals empowers them. It gives that extra boost that takes them from a wish to a determined path you plan to take. In 1953, one famous study focused on a graduating class from Yale University. The study concluded that the 3% of graduates that had written down their goals accumulated more wealth than the other 97% of the class combined.

Where you write your goals is totally up to you! You can type them up in a computer file or you can create a goal book and note them there. Experts say that handwritten goals and affirmations carry more weight because they involve more of your body's focus and effort, but the key is to write the goal and keep track of it.

EXERCISE: List three specific, major goals you have with respect to writing.

BREAK IT DOWN

"Shoot for the moon. Even if you miss, you'll land amongst the stars." --Les Brown

How do you eat an elephant? One bite at a time, right? Okay, none of us are going to be eating elephants anytime soon, but you get the picture. So many of our goals are *huge*. Let's face it, the process of selling a book, or losing 10 (or more) pounds, or getting out of the mid-list (where your books sell fine but not in huge numbers) are not one-shot deals. They take work, and the easiest way to do the work is to break it down into smaller, manageable steps.

Say your goal is to sell a book. Here are the steps Tawny personally used to break this goal down. Your steps might vary, of course.

- Choose a genre/sub-genre.

- Research what sub-genres are selling in Romance.
- Analyze my own writing to see where my voice and style fits.
- Investigate which houses/editors are buying and what their requirements are. Compile a list to refer back to.
- Consider ways to make *this* book stand out, or be different from all the others already doing well in this sub-genre or currently being submitted.
- Plot/outline/pantz the book (Because I'm a plotter, I always start with a plotting party and create an outline. Pantzers would probably just dive in.)
- Create a writing schedule. (Make it a livable schedule. Writing, like exercise, is something that's best done on a steady, regular basis.)
- Create benchmarks for the schedule to keep myself encouraged and focused.
- Add rewards - chocolate is always good.
- Write.
- And write some more.
- And write even more.
- And keep writing.
- Get feedback. Could be via critique groups or partners, contests or editor/agent feedback.
- Revise if necessary.
- Submit.
- Go back to that list of houses/editors I investigated and submit to as many houses/agents as I feel comfortable with.
- Use any feedback received from submissions, then submit some more.
- Start a new book. Always, always start a new book.

This same breakdown process can be applied to other goals, from going back to school to losing weight. Isabel Santos, Tawny's heroine in her January 2008 Blaze, *Does She Dare?*, applied this exact same process to get herself a man!

The key is to look at your goal and figure out how to make it manageable. For some people, the breakdown would be bigger steps (write, submit, write, submit). For others, the steps might be broken down even more. Everyone will have a slightly different method, of course, but the advantages of breaking your big goals into smaller steps are many:

You can easily track how close you are to making that dream into a reality.

If you find yourself frustrated with what seems a lack of progress, you can pinpoint where you need to focus (i.e., submissions not getting good responses? Go back to step one and research your sub-genre again to figure out why yours doesn't fit. Or possibly get more feedback through contests or critiques to see what area you can work on improving).

Smaller steps can help keep you focused and keep away feelings of discouragement. There are far more reasons to celebrate when you take it in small steps--and celebrations are one of the best ways to stay encouraged and focused on the big picture!

EXERCISE: Breakdown your three major goals into manageable steps.

PUT IT ON THE CLOCK

"There is no scarcity of opportunity to make a living at what you love; there's only scarcity of resolve to make it happen."

---Wayne Dyer

A goal needs a timeframe. This is actually one of the most important steps in goal setting. Without a "when" to be done by, it's just a lovely idea you want to happen "someday." Once you put a "due-by" date on the wish, then it's a goal.

So, how do you put it on the clock? First of all, look at your goal and ask yourself what the big picture due date is.

Tawny had a goal to sell by 2005. Of course, she always *hoped* it would happen earlier, but that was her deadline. (She sold in May 2006, which we'll cover in the last step, ALWAYS HAVE A BACKUP.)

To decide on this deadline, she did a little research and found that on *average* (again, mileage will vary) many writers took four years of serious writing to sell their first book. Kind of like college, right? She figured she was serious and she was doing everything she could to make it happen (i.e., she was working the steps she'd broken down, taking classes and workshops, using feedback, submitting). Because selling a book is such a huge step, she'd actually factored in a number of smaller accomplishments she wanted to achieve as well, such as finaling in local contests and the Golden Heart.

So what kind of time frame will you put on your goals? First decide what your deadline is for the big goal, then work backward. You've already broken them down into steps--look at each step and ask when you can reasonably complete it. Reasonableness is the key here. If you're working full-time with kids to run here and there, you might not have as much time to focus on writing as someone with fewer commitments. (Note, however, this is not an excuse not to write. If you want to, you'll find the time. Just be realistic about how much time that will be.)

If you've already sold and are trying to reach the next level, you'll have to factor in current writing and promotional deadlines. Real life is less intrusive if you make allowances for it in the beginning. Give yourself time for holidays and family commitments. Realize that some things are out of your hands, like editor response times. You want your timeframe to be realistic, but still challenging.

Once you've set your deadlines, be sure to read your goals regularly. Keep your calendar where you can see it. Don't put it in a drawer and forget it, or you'll lose that building momentum that will help make it come true. If you miss a deadline, revisit how that will affect the big picture and ask yourself what elements factored in. Was it because you just didn't feel like writing or was it because you were in the hospital? Was it because you waffled on submitting or was it because the editor was backlogged and took nine months to get back to you instead of the standard five?

Keep these elements in mind if you revise the deadlines. They're great tools to help analyze if the goal is one you'll work for (or are working for) or if you just like the sound of it.

EXERCISE: List what you want to have accomplished each month for the upcoming year.

IT'S ALL ABOUT SUPPORT

"Keep away from those who try to belittle your ambitions. Small people always do that, but the really great make you believe that you too can become great." – Mark Twain

We might dream alone, but dreams are easier to achieve with support. Friends, colleagues, family-- everyone you deal with will play a part in your goal achievements. Either they'll help build your confidence (give you support and believe in you, and offer feedback and ideas) or they'll tear you down (not respecting your time or when you say no, offering passive-aggressive (or all out aggressive) comments that chip away at your confidence, or belittling your dream). Even indifference may hurt you.

Take a look around and ask yourself where the people closest to you fall. Do they make you feel good? Like you can catch the moon? Or do they make you doubt your chances or feel unworthy? Your support team is all about the people who make you feel great. People who help you feel like you *can* have all your dreams come true. These are the ones you want to share your goals with and enlist for support. It could be a critique partner, a weight loss buddy, a family member or teacher. It could be one person or ten.

This is your team--who do you want on it? Once you've decided, go talk to them. Tell them about your goals, and share your timeframe and breakdown steps. Let them know what they can do to help you see this dream come true. In return, maybe you can do the same for them.

Once you've decided whom you want on your team, ask yourself what's missing. Do you have a great cheering section, but need help honing your craft? Perhaps you'd like a mentor on your team, or a series of workshop instructors who can help you grow and encourage you.

Think about it. Even if the perfect person to fill that empty team spot isn't already in your life, just keep an eye out. Once you define the job description, you'll be amazed at how fast you find someone to fill it.

Always remember two things, though. First, support is a two-way street. Second, no team in the world can make our dreams come true for us--only we have that power.

The bottom line is we have to support and believe in ourselves. We are each our team's captain and everyone will take their cues from how dedicated we are to motivating ourselves toward our goals. We're the ones with the most at stake, after all. Because if we give up, we're the ones who pay the price. Excuses might let you off the hook with others, but the bottom line is-- when you give up on your dream, you're the one who loses.

EXERCISE: Who's on *your* team?   List each team member's name, his support role, and how you'll ask for help with your goals.

ALWAYS HAVE A BACKUP

"Stay committed to your decisions, but stay flexible in your approach." --Tony Robbins

Reality is a tricky thing and, even when we're doing what we need to do in order to pursue our goals, our goals can still be derailed. The trick is not to give up.

When she first started writing, Tawny hoped to sell to Harlequin Temptation. She was really close to making that happen when the line closed. She had to regroup and rethink her goal. She refocused and shifted to her new goal—sell to Harlequin Blaze.

Tawny's original "big" goal was to sell by the end of 2005. That was a reasonable timeframe. She did all the right stuff. Took the workshops, entered the contests, listened to the feedback, and did all she could to improve her writing craft. And then came the end of 2005 and she hadn't achieved her goal.

Was it time to give up? She looked at her goals, written on an index card tacked next to her monitor, and had to decide: How reasonable was the dream? Was she on track? Were there indications that it *could* come true if she kept working? Definitely.

Did she want the dream or didn't she?

Of course she did, so she revised her timeline and stuck it out. Five months later, she sold to her dream editor.

When your goal shifts, regroup. Take into account your big picture and ask yourself how you can still have it. If your goal is to sell to a specific editor and that editor leaves publishing, how can you adjust? Find a new editor, of course.

The key to making your dreams into reality is to stay flexible. Like any good writer knows, revision is part of the process. That goes for your goals, too.

You might find you need to change the goal more drastically. Maybe the paranormal market is dead and you have to decide if you want to focus on the historical or the suddenly revitalized romantic comedy market.

You might find you need to revise your timeline. Or the steps of your game plan might have to be reconsidered. Be open to change. Even if you don't actively focus on your goals on a daily or weekly basis (i.e., you don't read your goal list and check your calendar to see if you're on track) checking in quarterly is a great idea. You'll be surprised to find how much you achieved. Once you start checking goals off your list, then you can add more goals and steps.

If your dreams are worth having, they are worth making a reality.

THINGS TO ASK YOURSELF IF YOU'RE
NOT MEETING YOUR WRITING GOALS

- How much time are you actually spending writing versus "learning to write?"
- How many projects are you working on at one time?
- How many people are reading your work? Offering feedback?
- Is what you are writing something that is marketable at the moment?
- How much attention are you paying to grammar, format, and guidelines?
- Are you being a "lazy" writer by doing the easy thing or are you challenging yourself to do the hard stuff?
- Are you listening to those with more experience?
- Is your ego preventing you from revising or cutting?
- Are you reading what you're writing?
- Are you reading what's currently selling?
- Are you treating your writing like a business and your story as a product that people are going to pay good money for?
- Are you taking rejection/criticism personally?
- What do you do after you receive rejection/criticism?
- Are you seeking help when you need it?
- What are you giving up to write? Can you give up something else?

CHAPTER 4

SEE JANE SCORE[8]:

DOING THE PREP WORK SO YOU CAN SCORE BIG

STEP 2: READ, EXPERIMENT AND

FAMILIARIZE YOURSELF WITH THE "10 FOR 10"

"First say to yourself what you would be and then do what you have to do." --Epictetus, Greek Philosopher

So you have a story idea. It could be about a character, place or situation. Something you've observed, heard or read about. Something you've lived or imagined. Whatever it is, you want to write it down. Maybe even share it.

How should you go about doing this?

It depends on what you're trying to accomplish. There are many ways to write a novel: organic (naturally, as it comes to you) or structured, consistent or sporadic, circular or linear. Writers instinctively gravitate towards one style. If you've had any amount of success (whether that means just finishing a novel, self-publishing it, or selling it to a New York publisher), you might be inclined to go with the "tried and true." However, what happens when your success falters? What if you get bored and want to try writing something new? What if further success doesn't come fast enough?

---

8   *See Jane Score* by Rachel Gibson

Needs and methods change, by chance or by design. Everyone, no matter where they are in their careers, can benefit from seeing how others approach craft.

Now, is "craft" synonymous with "rules?" We have been told at many workshops that a writer must first know the rules before she can break them. In our opinion, there are no "rules" when it comes to writing your story. What look like "rules" are only options previously used to successfully engage readers.

For example, we're fans of commas and periods. They certainly serve a purpose, as do other rules of grammar. In addition, certain publishers have "rules" specific to a target market or line. However, writers have been known to break grammar rules by writing in stream of consciousness or eliminating punctuation to create a certain effect. In addition, publishers have been known to deviate from established guidelines in order to expand a line with something they consider particularly brilliant.

Nonetheless, familiarizing yourself with established methods gives you the power to experiment and make reasoned decisions. Learn, then go with what feels right. Bottom line, why limit yourself?

Know yourself. Know your options. And know what your current needs are.

The first step to knowing your options is knowing whether you are writing commercial/genre fiction.

Virna didn't truly understand the distinction between commercial and literary fiction until she read Mary Buckham and Dianna Love's Break Into Fiction®:11 Steps to Building a Story that Sells. They explained that literary fiction is based on the reader's belief system that one cannot change their world but they can understand it better.

On the other hand, commercial or genre fiction (in addition to sharing a common narrative structure) tracks the striving of a central character as he or she overcomes obstacles to achieve a goal. The story ends on a positive note of some sort. Through his or her struggle, the character affects personal, positive internal character growth and changes himself, which can make a change in the world for the better.

Romance is commercial, genre fiction. If what you want is to write a romance novel and get it published, read what you want to write. This doesn't mean you need to imitate other writers or even follow any set process, but genre fiction follows a formula, which in turn creates reader expectation. If you hope to compete with other authors in the same genre, you need to know what they are doing and decide whether you are going to do the same thing or something just as good, only different.

In addition to reading other authors who write in your genre, you might want to explore different methods for writing your story. If your natural instinct is to jump right in and write, that's great. However, it doesn't always have to work that way. Some people "prepare" to write.

People who plot are often called "plotters," and there are a variety of tools they use, including plotting boards, post-it notes, spreadsheets, index cards, and writing journals. They may even collage before they start writing, collecting magazine pages or found objects that remind them of their imagined characters or plot points, and serve as inspiration during the writing process.

Tawny is a plotter. She needs to know her characters' goals and motivations before she starts writing. She also needs a workable plot, with a solid *Inciting Incident* that provides enough conflict to carry the story to the *Climax* (we'll explain these terms a little later, but you can also look in the glossary at the back of this book). What comes between those two events, though, is often a surprise. Despite that, she does do a plotting board, roughing out scene ideas and major emotional changes the characters need to experience.

Does her final product look like her initial plotting board? Rarely. But having the map frees up her mind to focus on the story.[9]

Some writers, on the other hand, find outlining represses their creativity because it tells them how the story is going to play out, and they want to discover details about character and plot as they write. They prefer the element of surprise and unknown possibilities. These types of writers are commonly referred to as "pantzers," because they tend to write by the seat of their pants.

Virna is a reformed pantzer. She wrote her first two manuscripts with no specific structure in mind. And even though they were good enough to get her a great agent, she now knows they could have been better.

Virna tells a little about her transition from pantzer to pantzer/plotter here:

When I started writing, I needed to realize my creative possibilities. I knew following guidelines would stifle and intimidate me. So I didn't pay attention to rules or even what the market was asking for. I loved reading romantic suspense, so that's what I wrote.

The upside was that I immediately connected with the writer inside me and confirmed I did have stories to tell. Passion motivated me to write and meet other writers. This gave me unbelievable momentum. I threw myself into my writing and within three months I had pitched to an editor, finished my first manuscript, and got signed by an agent.

The downside of jumping into writing was that when my first manuscript didn't sell, I didn't know what to do next. The same editors who told me I wrote well, had an engaging voice, and

---

[9] It was only through years of trial and error that she found the right tools that let her create a strong enough map to write, but didn't stifle her creative flow. Like all creative endeavors, she believes it's through trial and error that we can truly free ourselves to write.

created intriguing plots and characters also rejected my manuscript because it ultimately wasn't "compelling" enough to stand out in an impacted market.

Not compelling enough. That was it. No explanation of what that meant. No guidance on how to fix it. My agent reassured me this was just part of the business and to concentrate on writing the next novel. But I had to decide how I was going to do that. Would I again go with my instincts and assume I could fix whatever had gone "wrong" the first time? I saw that as potential waste of time.

I needed creative freedom to start writing, but I didn't want to keep writing book after book with no idea whether I was any closer to getting published. That being said, I'd learned a lot about craft, but not enough to come up with an overall game plan or process. All that changed when I learned about several key concepts and their connection to one another.

In the following section, we expand upon these concepts.

THE "10 FOR 10" TRIANGLE

"10 for 10" refers to the coincidence of there being 10 Steps in Part I of this book with this step (step 2) discussing what are, in our opinion, the 10 most basic but important concepts in writing.

Jennifer Crusie once said that plot can be envisioned as an inverted triangle because your first line "eliminates 99% of the choices" and these choices continue to diminish as the story continues. Everything in the plot leads to the last scene, which is critical to the structure of the entire story.

This triangle analogy also works well for describing how Story incorporates 10 interrelated writing concepts. The "10 For 10" triangle illustrates from top to bottom the progression of Story, starting with the largest, most inclusive principles and working towards the more detailed and unique aspects of a story, including individual scenes and the story's resolution. As you work down the triangle, the next element will always subsume and be affected in some way by what came before.

Imagine that the top of the inverted triangle represents the two "biggest" and "broadest" components of your story: Theme and Story Question. (Note: this does not mean you have to nail down your Theme before you start writing. Most people won't know their true Theme until they start writing. Rather, it illustrates that every component listed below Theme will be used to prove your Theme.) The rest of the triangle is devoted to the framework and individual components of your story—everything you need to prove *your* Theme and answer *your* Story Question is funneled through the top of the triangle.

The components of Story are physical and emotional. The building blocks are: 1) Who (Characters); 2) What (Plot); 3) Where (Setting/Location); 4) When (Setting/Time); and 5) Why (Intent). These building blocks are not just dumped into the triangle at random. Rather, they are placed with deliberation. They may be moved around a lot, but they'll still eventually find their place in the Story.

After 1) Theme and 2) Story Question comes: 3) Character; 4) Conflict; and 5) Plot, which are discussed individually, but actually work in concert. The next five components are: 6) Three Act Structure; 7) Turning Points; 8) Raised Stakes/Options Narrow; 9) Scene versus Sequel; and 10) Goal/Happy Ending. Finally, subsumed within these ten Story components is the concept of *Character Arc* (as well as other principles that will be discussed) because Character Arc attaches to the main characters and develops throughout the story.

By familiarizing yourself with these concepts, they will find their way into your writing process whether you consciously think of them or not. It's all about having the tools and options to write *your* story in whatever way you choose to.

Below is a diagram of the "10 For 10" triangle. If you have trouble distinguishing the individual elements because of the limited sizing of this book, you can find the triangle at www.lovewritingbook.com.

"10 FOR 10" – Diagram 1

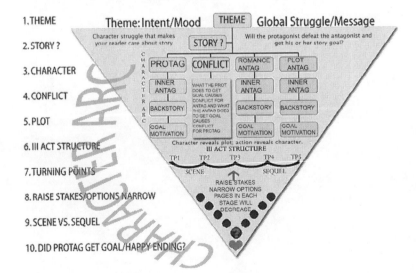

You May Be A Romance Writer If...

- You have a subscription to Publisher's Weekly or bug a friend who does.
- You know the difference between a WIP, an MS, and an HEA.
- You go to "chapter" meetings.
- You've heard of NaNoWriMo. You might have tried it. You might even have completed it.
- You are shocked at how much money some authors make and how little money others do.
- You pay people to reject you (contests).
- You view a request for revisions as a minor miracle.
- People reject you for free (queries).
- You're surprised when people don't reject you.
- You proudly display your first rejection and tell others about it so you can become a "PRO."

CHAPTER 5

THEME

Did you know?   Theme is what gives your story universal meaning.

Theme touches everything in a story even though it is only one element among many.   But what is it?   According to the dictionary, it's a topic of discourse, but that's not very helpful, is it?   Really, Theme is about giving purpose and meaning to your story at the same time you entertain your readers.   Meaning can be found in tone, in individual words, in concepts and imagery, and in broad messages, subtle or not.   When crafted deliberately, Theme shelters or exposes your characters and gives significance to their actions.

Generally, Theme represents an underlying truth--a view about life and how people behave that establishes a common ground with your reader.   It is the "global" hook that tells the reader why he should read your story, and it encompasses the story hook--that is, the reason why the reader will be interested in the actions, growth, and fate of your specific characters.

Theme can be broken down in two ways.   First, as Bob Mayer puts it, Theme manifests your intent in writing a novel.   What global message and mood do you want to impart?   How do you want your reader to feel?   With romance, the reader expectation is an affirmation of love in the form of a happy ending, but there can be several ways to get there.   Will your reader be exposed to the darker side of life, or will you make the drive a light and funny one?   Will you try to incorporate both?   Make an informed choice because your thematic intent will be obvious from the very first line of your novel. It is a promise to the reader that, once made, can't be taken back.

Word choice, imagery and symbolism, and concepts will all affect the tone and mood of your book, and thus your readership. If a reader opens your book and reads a first line indicating a dark intent (maybe your first scene is written in the point of view ("POV") of a psychotic killer), she might not be in the mood for dark—even if a happy ending is waiting. Likewise, if a reader is struggling with difficult issues, maybe she won't appreciate a snarky, funny tone, even if she normally would. You can't control reader mood or preferences, but you can control the mood of your book, make a reasoned decision, and tell the story you need to tell.

Second, Theme posits a global question to the reader, with you asserting (and supporting) a particular conclusion about life and humanity. Yes, your characters say and do "XY&Z" to get to the happy ending, but the result shouldn't be random—it should be based on some greater principal that will apply to the majority of people, not just the characters within the covers of your book. Theme does this by focusing the story on a global struggle faced by mankind. The struggle rests on something important that most likely transcends time and culture--something visceral and compelling that speaks to mankind's basic needs. It gives answers to questions your readers are probably already asking, thus giving them another reason to identify with your story and your characters.

For example, in *Chosen By Blood*, the first book of Virna's paranormal romantic suspense series, the Theme is "In order to live a fulfilled life, one must balance duty with desire. " Given this type of thematic message, a message that almost any reader can relate to, the reader's continued participation in the story will probably be motivated both by self-interest and a genuine interest in your characters' fate.

Sometimes you might not recognize your thematic message until you've brainstormed characters and plot, but that's okay. With this writing method, you will revisit Theme, as well as different ways to thread Theme throughout your book, in different ways. At some point, however, you should have your thematic message firmly in mind because you can powerfully yet subtly prove your message in every scene you write, thus subconsciously reinforcing its importance to your reader.

For ideas on thematic messages, look to biblical literature, mythology, or universal concepts (such as the seven deadly scenes or seven virtues). For example, you might want to explore greed, one of the seven deadly sins, and whether loving a person means being willing to give up all material possessions for them. Or you might play with the notion of "judgment" as illustrated in the Bible to explore why true intimacy isn't possible until judgment is exchanged for compassion, in particular self-compassion. Finally, you might use mythic stories to form a Theme about resistance, and how resisting Fate is often the very thing that leads a person to fall prey to it. We're not saying your book will refer, explicitly or implicitly, to religion, sin, or mythology at all, but you can use these larger philosophical tenants to develop a global message for your reader and to develop a plot.

Study how concepts, beliefs, superstitions, or behaviors impact mankind. Form a conclusion (for example, that acceptance leads to happiness, but resistance leads to disaster), state this conclusion early in your story (you can use subtext or even have a character comment on his/her beliefs regarding the Theme), and spend the rest of your story trying to prove you're right.

That being said, try not to lecture. You need to walk a fine line between imparting a message and ramming your individual morays down a reader's throat. Readers want to be entertained and informed, maybe even challenged to a certain extent, but few want to defend their political or religious choices when reading genre fiction.

EXERCISE:

    1. List three universal concepts from which you can build a Theme. Example: Crime; Loyalty; Friendship

2. For each of these concepts, make a thematic assertion. Example: *Crime doesn't pay; Loyalty can be carried too far; Family does not always trump friendship.*

3. Choose the one thematic assertion that speaks to you the most and reword it so the essence of your thematic assertion is phrased as follows: In order to be happy, one must _____.

4. Example: *In order to be happy, one must believe that goodness is rewarded and crime is punished.*

5. Think of a character (but make it someone a reader can ultimately root for) who might not believe in your thematic assertion. Example: *A successful thief or a victim of a crime.*

6. Describe how this character could end up proving the thematic assertion true. Make sure that in order to prove your thematic assertion true, the sympathetic character must defeat another character in some way. Example: *A redeemed thief helps bring down the criminal organization he'd previously been involved with or a woman helps apprehend the husband who tried to kill her.*

7. Analyze the mood of the story you just described. Is it a light, funny story or a darker, edgier one? Either way, describe a story that proves the thematic assertion true, but this time by targeting the opposite kind of mood. Example: *A 10-year-old thief accidentally left home alone for the holidays prevents robbers from getting into his house.*

CHAPTER 6

STORY QUESTION

Did you know? The answer to your Story Question is justified by your Theme.

In addition to proving a stated Theme, Story serves another "big" purpose by answering a novel's central Story Question — "Will the protagonist (the main character who changes the most in your story) defeat the antagonist (the character that most gets in the way of what your main character wants) and get his or her story goal?"

We will be looking at all these concepts in much more detail, but right now, focus on the question. It's the question that identifies and brings to life the components of *your* story (the main characters, their competing goals, their actions, and the result of their ensuing contemplation and reactions). It also exemplifies why writing commercial, genre fiction (fiction that follows a formula in order to meet reader expectation), and in particular *romantic fiction* (fiction that has a happy ending), is so difficult.

Since romance comes with a happy ending and readers expect the protagonist to "win," romance writers   have to craft their story so well that the answer to the Story Question isn't obvious (otherwise there is no suspense or tension to keep the reader interested) but only makes sense upon retrospection. In effect, romance writers want to make the reader forget the outcome she's expecting, and then rejoice when she actually gets it.

In the "10 For 10" triangle, the eight story components that come after Theme and Story Question exist under the shadow of these two broader elements. We've heard many authors (including Mary Buckham and Bob Mayer) refer to Theme and Story Question as a foundation, and the remaining components as the framework of a house. We think of Theme and Story Question as a puppeteer's handle, and everything else as the strings and puppet itself. Theme and Story Question breathe life into the story, just as the puppeteer breathes life into the puppet.

Your story components *prove* your Theme. In addition, each story component is introduced simply as a means to answer the Story Question. As the tip of the story triangle narrows, your main character, the protagonist, will move faster and faster towards his "goal" (the thing he wants) with his choices becoming fewer and fewer. Pacing intensifies. Character growth spikes. Stakes rise. All of this pushes the reader to continually ask:

Will the protagonist defeat the antagonist and get his goal at the end of your story?

The answer to this question is going to be justified by your Theme. In other words, everything in the story, including how the story ends, should serve to prove your thematic assertion true. In a romance, since we know the protagonist is going to get a happy ending, that happy ending is only going to come about because the protagonist has learned and lived the lesson of your Theme.

EXERCISE:

1. Based on the previous exercise, use one of the stories you described to prove your thematic assertion true and list three things your sympathetic character (protagonist) and the character he/she defeats (antagonist) might want. Example: *The woman whose husband tried to kill her might want: to save her sister, to find love again, to live in peace; the husband who tried to kill her might want: to kill her sister (and then her when he discovers she's still alive), information, or revenge.*

2. Now, using the list you created above, pick one thing the sympathetic (protagonist) character and other character (antagonist) each wants and reword your

story description so the conclusion is in the form of a question. Example: *Will the heroine defeat the husband who tried to kill her (and who now wants revenge), and get her goal of saving her sister's life?*

You May Be A Romance Writer If...

- You hide when an outgoing "board" member from your chapter walks by.
- You try to beat out hundreds of others for a decent pitch appointment but end up throwing your computer against the wall when you can't sign on to the RWA website.
- You feel proud when you can stand in the buffet line next to an editor or agent and act like a cool, non-desperate human being.
- You'll stop reading an author because you've met him/her at a writing event and had a bad experience.
- You spend a lot of money on raffle tickets.
- When your husband asks "Weren't you just at a conference," you look at him blankly and say, in all seriousness, "Yeah. So?"
- You're willing to hang out with smokers in order to make contacts.
- -One of your personal heroes is named Nora.
- You've thought about crashing the Harlequin party (although of course you never have!)
- Your "to be read" pile quadruples after July.

CHAPTER 7

CHARACTER

Did you know? Your characters are the vehicles with which you prove your Theme and answer your Story Question.

Previously, we talked about proving Theme and answering Story Question. In order to do both, you will need characters.

Characters are the heart and soul of any novel. After all, what is a story if not events that *happen* to and affect characters? Readers read because they want to be entertained, but also because they want to feel and be touched on a deep level by what is happening to your characters. The best way to accomplish this is to have complex, fully developed characters that reveal themselves in the story so that the reader cares about who the story is affecting.

In generating a story idea, you might ask yourself what type of character you want to write about. Sometimes this will come naturally if you have a distinctive plot in mind (i.e., a suspense or thriller will usually have characters involved in law enforcement or the military). It's crucial, however, to then take these character "types," (a broad, generic description; i.e., teenager, librarian, vampire, etc), and mold them into something more.

Characters should be multi-dimensional and unpredictable. Yet, they must also have human qualities that readers will relate to. Either way, you need to go further than "typing" your character. You must also consider what it is about these characters that will make a reader care about whether they get their goal or not. They will need a past, a present, and dreams for the future. They will need flaws and attributes, hobbies, quirks, and a distinct way of speaking.

A complex, fully developed character is one that "seems real" to the reader--someone the reader can identify with, understand, or be intrigued with. It is someone shaped by past experiences and well-motivated to change (or not change in the case of the antagonist).

If you write a story with a villain who kills someone on every page, but you don't give the reader any information about the villain, why will your reader care? Likewise, even if your story is exclusively about robots, those robots must possess at least some human qualities and characteristics in order for the reader to relate to them. And finally, even if you purposefully craft an unlikable character, that character must be someone the reader is willing to spend time with, and this means he must be well-motivated.

For example, in the movie *Law Abiding Citizen*, Gerard Butler plays a man on a murderous rampage, killing not only criminals, but honest, hard-working innocents, as well. However, even though viewers might not like his character, they understand he's well-motivated because he's avenging the violent murders of his own wife and child, as well as what he views as a miscarriage of justice by the very people he trusted to represent them.

To fully explore characters, we are going to focus on three things: identifying major characters, creating memorable characters, and revealing complex characters.

IDENTIFYING MAJOR CHARACTERS

PROTAGONIST

Every story has a protagonist because every story is "owned" by one of the main characters. This person is the subject of your Story Question. It is the character around which the story revolves. It is the character that is trying to achieve something in your story, and the person who grows and changes the most because of the events of the story.

This person's life is not perfect, even if he/she thinks it is. At the very beginning of the story (some say even the first page), something is going to happen to shake up the protagonist's world. This is often referred to as the *Inciting Incident* that gives the protagonist a shove out of his/her *Ordinary World*.

ANTAGONIST

Every story also has an antagonist. This is the person, thing, or situation that creates the initial conflict resulting in the Inciting Incident. The antagonist forces the protagonist into action towards a particular goal (usually not in a positive way), but then the antagonist continues to act in order to prevent the protagonist from getting what he wants.

While a story only has one protagonist, it can have multiple antagonists. In Diagram 1 of the "10 For 10" triangle, we have characterized these three types of antagonists as External (another person, a force of nature, etc), Internal (the conflicts created by a person's own beliefs or back story), and Romantic (the conflicts caused by a romantic interest). Every character, not just the protagonist, can face these antagonists in your story, but the external antagonist is the one that causes the most obvious trouble for your protagonist.

ROMANTIC INTEREST

A romance always has a character that serves as your protagonist's romantic interest. This person is always going to be a kind of "romantic antagonist" for the protagonist. Otherwise, there would be no suspense to the romantic plot. This is why the romantic interest is usually the worst romantic partner for the protagonist. She will represent what the protagonist both secretly wants and fears most. Usually this person has the ability to provide the protagonist what he needs in his life to be whole.

For example, in the movie *Romancing The Stone*, the character of Joan Wilder longs for passion and adventure, but she thinks what she needs is her nice safe life in NY. Jack, the hero, is determined to take her off the road and into the jungle itself, swinging on vines over an abyss; even worst, he wants the map and treasure, which is what Joan is supposed to use to ransom her kidnapped sister with.

SECONDARY CHARACTERS

These are characters that interact with your major characters or act around them. The role of secondary characters is often to shed light on the protagonist, either because they know information the reader doesn't or because they prod the protagonist to act and make choices, which is going to reflect on who the protagonist is.

A secondary character must serve a purpose and a "subplot" (a second plot in the story taking place at the same time of the main plot) must tie directly to the main plot to be relevant. (A "subplot" is crucial to the events in the main plot; a "secondary plot" is one that stands on its own but gives significance or meaning to the main plot.) Also beware of introducing too many characters in the story, especially at the beginning of the book. The main focus should be on the protagonist. If the reader has to wonder who the protagonist of the story is, or if the reader likes your protagonist's buddy more than the protagonist himself, you may be in trouble

As Lori Wilde says,

"While you need more characters to get a bigger book feel, too many characters bogs the story down and the reader has trouble keeping up with who everyone is. Also, if you give characters multiple roles, it gives the book a bigger feel and makes it more efficient."

Also remember that if you give a character POV scenes (a scene viewed directly through her eyes), the reader might expect that character to be crucial to the main plot and is going to want to see that character go through some kind of Character Arc.

When you create your list of main characters in Step 3, you might want to look at your character list and ask if any of the characters can serve the same function as another (i.e., mentor another character, act as a red herring, reveal the back story of another character). Then get rid of the extraneous characters. Likewise, when you emphasize particular character traits, try to give them a purpose in the story. Show how a quirk or flaw or attribute reveals and deepens characterization, but also how it directly affects the plot. Otherwise, you've emphasized something that has no real meaning in the story.

CREATING MEMORABLE CHARACTERS

Memorable characters are ones you remember long after a book or movie is over. They are dynamic and relatable, yet have hidden complexities.

For example, did you know that Smurfette was created to infiltrate the Smurf Village and was originally unattractive and annoying? She underwent a character transformation aided by magic and the help of her new Smurf friends (what we call Character Arc).

In a work of fiction, memorable characters should be S-M-U-R-F-A-B-L-E: Sympathetic, Motivated, Unique, Redeemable, Flawed, Active, Believable, Layered, and Experienced.

Let's take a quick look at what each of these terms mean when applied to fictional characters:

- Sympathetic: looked upon with favor or compassion; to feel an affinity for; this is what makes your reader relate to your character, be it the protagonist or the antagonist

- Motivated: to feel an incentive or reason to act, which will make your characters' actions in the story both compelling and believable (see "believable" below)

- Unique: to make distinctive (think: physical characteristics or mannerisms, speech, background, skills, profession, etc), which makes your characters interesting and stand apart from others

- Redeemable: capable of being set free, rescued, restored, or ransomed (as in honor, worth, or reputation) [think capable of undergoing change]. Note: most antagonists are not redeemed at the end, but some of the most interesting ones make you believe they might be redeemable during the story

- Flawed: having an imperfection, defect or shortcoming, which makes your characters interesting, relatable, and have someplace to go through the events of the plot

- Active: being in physical motion, which is interesting and engaging and results in more conflict and change

- Believable: credible, apparently reasonable, which keeps your reader engaged

- Layered: having depth (includes tension, strengths & weaknesses, secrets, etc), which makes your characters, and thus your plot, more complex

- Experienced: knowledgeable as a result of active participation; one who is experienced in life is going to have a back story that impacts who she is today; she will have dreams, fears, shadows, Incorrect Core Beliefs etc

Let's look at some examples to see how these elements have been portrayed in well-known characters:

Example: Luke Skywalker (*Star Wars*)

- Sympathetic: He's an orphan living with his aunt and uncle; he's a dreamer who wants more than to be a farmer

- Motivated: He longs for adventure; wants to avenge the death of his family/help Rebel Alliance/redeem his father from evil that controls him

- Unique: He repairs robots and his father was a Jedi knight

- Redeemable: He has a strong sense of duty and a desire to be a part of something larger than himself; he obeys his aunt and uncle even though he's resentful

- Flawed: He's emotional and impulsive/romantic, dreamy, naïve (he races off after R2 without telling his uncle and he spies on the Sand People, almost getting himself killed)

- Active: He goes off to find Princess Leia and teams up with Obi One

- Believable: His growth is shown over the Star Wars trilogy, not all at once; he doesn't become the confident hero overnight, but has to go through a series of lessons and tests with Yoda, flounders at first; he's not the suave buccaneer that Han Solo is.

- Layered: His father is his arch enemy, he has a long lost sister, his friends are robots

- Experienced (as in, has a history that impacts who he is today): He has a father he doesn't know much about other than he was a Jedi knight, he grew up yearning for more than the simple life he was living

Example: Vivian Ward (*Pretty Woman*)

- Sympathetic: She's independent, acts as her own agent, doesn't want a pimp, has a good friend, Kit, and they take care of each other, the shopping clerks in the movie treat her badly, Richard Gere's friend, Stuckey, treats her badly

- Motivated: She takes care of herself to survive; she has no skills to get another job even though tries; her roommate has spent the rent money on drugs

- Unique: She's a prostitute that looks like Julia Roberts, she's smart (she negotiates her fee to stay with Gere for a week), she doesn't have jaded hard edge or common vices

- Redeemable: We catch glimpses that she wants the fairytale and is a loyal friend (she visits her friend no matter what her current status says she should do), she's smart and won't let others take advantage of her, she's a good judge of character (doesn't like/trust Stuckey)

- Flawed: She's a prostitute, suffers from lack of confidence/self-worth, she's prejudiced/mistrusting
- Active: She tries to fit in/better herself for Edward, seeks help from hotel manager
- Believable: She is shunned by others who judge her, doesn't stick up for herself at first and is hurt by the way others view her
- Layered: She loves opera, is a loyal friend, is honest ("I would have stayed for two thousand"), is vulnerable (won't let him kiss her on mouth), is feisty but goodhearted, too
- Experienced: She has learned not to get emotional, tries to stay numb, charges Edward even to give him directions, mistrustful of Edward at first

Example: Martin Riggs (_Lethal Weapon_)
- Sympathetic: He's a cop on the edge after his wife is murdered
- Motivated: He has nothing left to lose, all he has is his job and his need for revenge
- Unique: He lapses into a Three Stooges routine, can dislocate his shoulder to get out of traps
- Redeemable: He has a sense of humor, he enjoys hassling his new partner (Danny Glover), he can't pull the trigger to kill himself
- Flawed: He jumps feet first into danger, he needs to be more cautious, he needs to let others get close to him
- Active: Being active is not a problem for the impulsive cop

- Believable: He visits his wife's grave, he's an alcoholic, he lives in a trailer

- Layered: He has a dog for a companion, he's a Three Stooges fan, his partner's family likes him, he has a sense of humor but is vulnerable

- Experienced: He loved his wife and is tormented by her death, he's always been a bit "out there" but he's a good cop

Example: Knox Devereaux (*Chosen By Blood* by Virna DePaul, Berkley 2011)

- Sympathetic: He's a half human/ half vampire who cares for his clan; he's very self-sacrificing

- Motivated: He's sworn to bring his clan back to health by finding an antidote for what ails them; leading a new special ops team is his chance to get it

- Unique: He's a vampire prince even though he's half-human, he can't lie, he wants to be monogamous when others in his race generally aren't, he has a scar above his lip

- Redeemable: He can't stay away from the human woman he loves despite the fact he should, he loves his mother and brother, he cares for those weaker than himself, he's a good father

- Flawed: He doesn't know how to balance duty and desire, he thinks poorly of humans in general

- Active: He agrees to lead a special ops team and he continues to pursue Felicia, the heroine

- Believable: He's deferential to the Vamp Council at beginning, he seeks his clan's approval, he slowly begins to care less about this

- Layered: He loves his wife and children, but thinks Felicia is his soul mate, he has a close relationship with his family, he has unsettled resentment against his father, he has many different skills/powers

- Experienced: He feels judged because of his father's mistakes, he's determined not to fail his clan like his father did, he believes his physical strength is the only reason his clan follows him, he feels he can't have love if it means marrying someone other than a vamp

REVEALING COMPLEX CHARACTERS

The way we reveal our characters is just as important as the way we create them. Ideally, you want to reveal them to your reader with a balance of internal narrative, dialogue and action. Try to use subtext and have your characters act unpredictably.

As J.A. Konrath states in *The Newbie's Guide To Publishing*, "Interesting characters are not interesting because of who they are. They are interesting because of what they do. Who they are might affect what they do...These actions and dialogs should be revealed through the plot."

Let's look at a particular situation: a man is in love with a woman about to marry his best friend. What are the ways you can reveal his feelings, but also who the man is by nature?

We can answer these questions by studying this particular situation in a movie, *Love Actually*. In this movie, Juliet and Peter are wed in a ceremony videotaped by Mark, Peter's best friend and best man. Mark is the man in love with his best friend's girlfriend, now wife. How was this revealed? By action and dialogue.

- Mark has always been cold and unfriendly to Juliet and tries to avoid her. (Revealing character through action.)
- When the professional wedding video turns out to be dreadful, Juliet shows up at Mark's door in hopes of getting a copy of his footage and tells him she wants to be friends with him. The video he recorded turns out to consist entirely of close-ups of her, and she realizes that he secretly has feelings for her. (Revealing character through action.)
- Mortified, Mark creates an excuse to leave and informs Juliet that his prior cold attitude towards her was "a self preservation thing." (Revealing character through dialogue.)

- He hesitates and almost goes back to the apartment several times to tell her how he feels, but he ultimately keeps walking. (In this scene, even if we didn't know how he felt about Juliet, his actions reveal how much he loves her but also how much he loves/respects his best friend.)

- In the movie, we don't see any internal narrative, but we can imagine what it would be. "I need to tell her how I feel. But I can't. Think of Peter. What that would do to him. But this is my last chance. Don't I deserve to be happy, too? Maybe she loves me back?"

- On Christmas Eve, Mark shows up at Juliet and Peter's door posing as a carol singer with a portable CD player, and uses a series of cardboard signs to silently tell her that "at Christmas you tell the truth," and, "without hope or agenda... to me, you are perfect." (Revealing character through action and pseudo dialogue.)

- As he leaves, Juliet runs after him and kisses him before returning to Peter. Mark tells himself, "Enough, enough now." (Revealing character through dialogue to himself.)

These examples illustrate the many varied ways you can reveal a character to a reader. In this same vein, let's look at how you can imbue your writing with the emotions of your characters.

EMOTION

In order to show your character's emotions, constantly ask yourself the following:

1. What is my character feeling right now?

2. Why are they feeling it? This is going to be influenced by your character's past and their current issues

3. How can I show what they are feeling? This is about showing, not telling. Specifically, you want to show emotion in a way that is consistent with your character's personalities. Show thoughts, feelings, and physical sensations. Don't use language that tells the reader what the character is feeling.

4. Consider whether your character has a "telling habit" whenever she feels a particular emotion. For example, a character might lapse into Spanish when she feels intimidated.

5. Finally, although you want to show what your character is thinking and physically feeling to convey emotion, you can also look at what they're doing and trying not to do. Struggling not to show emotion is emotional in and of itself. In addition, trying to distract oneself from grief by packing up a lover's things is an emotional action that the reader won't miss. Stepping back and making the emotion part of the background, as Alicia Rasley suggests, gives it greater impact. The emotion becomes an integral part of the scene that the reader can't ignore as easily as she could ignore or dismiss or run away from the tears and wails of a character in distress.

EXERCISE:

1. Consider why your sympathetic character (protagonist) does not initially believe in your thematic assertion. Example: Why doesn't the woman whose husband tried to kill her believe that goodness is rewarded and crime is punished? Because her father was a drug lord who was never apprehended; she also went to the cops when her husband was physically abusing her and they

did nothing to help her; her husband tried to kill her and escaped and is now after her sister.

2. Think of three strengths and weaknesses for your protagonist and antagonist. In particular, think of attributes that make your antagonist sympathetic to a reader. Example: The antagonist has a son he loves or a mother he always brings flowers to at the end of the week.

CHAPTER 8

CONFLICT

Did you know? Conflict is what forces your characters to reveal who they really are.

So now you should have some characters in mind, not just character types. You have characters your reader will care about. However, how are you going to keep your readers caring about your characters throughout an entire story? By giving your characters conflict.

WHAT IS CONFLICT?

Conflict is defined as "opposition in a work of drama or fiction between characters or forces (especially an opposition that motivates the development of the plot)."

Conflict (two forces in opposition) is naturally exciting. It challenges your characters and your readers are initially happiest when your characters are challenged. Why? Because they don't know what's going to happen next. It's the unknown possibilities that are exciting and engaging. After all, if you're writing a romance, your reader already has an expectation that the answer to the Story Question (will the protagonist defeat the antagonist?) will be "yes." However, what the reader doesn't know is *how* this will be achieved. What keeps your readers engaged with the story is their desire to see what your characters will do in the face of conflict.

According to Lori Wilde,

"Most books start with a bang because if you don't catch an editor or agent's interest in the first page, they'll stop reading. You don't want that. Some books do start out slower but if you start slower, your writing must be very compelling. Here's the real thing that holds the editors/agents interest--conflict. If you can put conflict on each and every page of your story, you've got it made."

In a romance, there are three types of conflict that a character faces.

Conflict can be:

- Internal Conflict: Emotional or *internal* struggles. This tells us how the character feels about a particular situation, belief, or compulsion, but often impacts how the character behaves. Therefore, a character's internal struggles can drive the plot;

- External Conflict: Situational or *external* struggles. Obviously, a character will outwardly react (or maybe consciously fail to act) in response to External Conflict. However, once again, how a character reacts to External Conflict often gives us insight into that character's emotional state or personality traits. Both External and Internal Conflict drive the character growth resulting in Character Arc; and

- Romantic Conflict: Romantic struggles. These are both *external* and *internal* struggles that directly impact a romantic relationship, drive character growth, and impact the external plot.

Let's take a look at how all these conflicts thread together in romantic fiction. (We'll be discussing these conflicts in greater detail in Chapter 12, when we analyze how each conflict has its own arc, and how these arcs track Character Arc in general.) In Tawny's September 2010 Blaze, *Riding The Waves*, the story opens with the heroine's emotional, Internal Conflict, front and center: she wants to experience a sexual adventure, but she's so worried about what other people think of her that she doesn't want to risk anyone finding out. As such, her goal at the beginning of the story is to have a vacation fling, far away from the judgment and prying eyes of the physics lab she works at. She wants a boy toy, a guy for pure pleasure and no commitments.

And she gets him.

However, when she gets home and back to the lab, she discovers that her new project leader and visiting dignitary is none other than her wild, sexy fling. Now, her internal and external goals are in direct conflict – she wanted a fling, but more importantly, she wanted to maintain her reputation and dignity by having the fling in secret.

This scenario creates 1) Internal Conflict – his presence is going to push her desires but she's not going to want to act on them because she thinks she has to maintain a certain image; 2) External Conflict – they're forced to work together but have different visions for the project they're working; and 3) Romantic Conflict – she's forced to interact with the hero, which is going to heighten her desire to be with him, but he's her boss and being with him is a huge conflict because it risks exposing their prior affair and destroying the reputation she values so much. Because of all these factors, the heroine is forced to face her internal fears and insecurities.

EXERCISE: Give your protagonist and antagonist an Internal Conflict and explain how these Internal Conflicts manifest themselves in their behavior. Example: *The antagonist believes a person only gets one soul mate per lifetime, so he rejects attempts by another woman to comfort him/talk him out of revenge; the heroine believes all a man could want from her is her money, so she only relies on people she feels she can buy, rather than people who simply want to help her.*

You May Be A Romance Writer If...

- You curse when your workshop proposal is rejected.
- You panic when your workshop proposal is accepted.
- You bring an extra suitcase with you to your annual conference.
- You mentally say "Oh, what the hell. Just talk to her," several times during a conference
- You're trying to decide between groceries and a workshop/contest fee/conference fee.
- You actually ask questions at workshops.
- You go up to [insert favorite author's name here] at a conference and squeal, "You're the reason I write romance," then immediately feel foolish before slinking away.
- At a conference, you find yourself groveling for attention from someone you don't even know but who everyone else seems determined to impress. You go up to your room to shower.
- You actually submit a manuscript after it's been requested.
- You check your email constantly for news on a submission and email yourself just to make sure it's working correctly.

CHAPTER 9

PLOT (CONFLICT BETWEEN PROTAGONIST AND ANTAGONIST FORCES ACTION)

Did you know? Your plot results from your characters repeatedly acting in response to conflict.

We have discussed characters and the three broad types of conflict found in a romance novel. Now, we're going to break conflict down even further by looking at how conflict forces your characters to act and, therefore, drives the series of events that make up your plot.

To briefly summarize, a story's major characters (protagonist and antagonist) face conflict on three levels: internal, external, and romantic. This makes your characters interesting and likable to your reader. This, however, isn't enough to sustain your reader's interest for a whole novel. You can create interesting characters, but if they spend the book walking around by themselves, thinking out loud and not doing anything about their conflicts, then your reader is probably going to lose interest pretty quick. To sustain interest, the reader needs action. How then, do you make your characters act?

With "action-inducing" conflict created by a series of "progressive complications."

Your characters, however, do not just act at whim. To answer your Story Question (Will the protagonist defeat the antagonist and get his/her story goal?), your character's actions must be focused in order to create your story's linear "plot."

What is "plot?" Plot is the external events of your story. More specifically, it is the action, and the cause and effect of this action, between your two most important characters that forces your protagonist to grow, answers the Story Question, and proves your Theme. You can also have a "subplot," which focuses on the actions of your secondary characters, but is still somehow crucial to your main plot.

In romantic fiction, the best conflict is action-inducing conflict because it not only forces your characters to act, but to grow. Just as your reader wants to see how your characters will act, she wants to see how the characters will adapt and learn and grow from beginning to end. Conflict that prods your character to act time and again makes for a more believable and engaging story.

Conflict motivates character growth because it motivates not only action, but reaction, introspection, exploration and adaptation. As such, consistent with this thinking, conflict should be defined as, "opposition in a work of drama or fiction between characters or forces (especially an opposition that motivates the development of the plot *and the growth of the characters*)." Conflict has the most meaning when it illustrates the emotional growth of your characters (or lack of growth, which is often the case with an antagonist).

As an aside, also remember that the change you want to see in your character should be consistent with or prove the Theme of your story (it can also disprove your Theme by contrast, but we'll discuss this more later). See how this is all threading together?

THE IMPORTANCE OF A WORTHY GOAL IN DEVELOPING CONFLICT

The first step to creating action-inducing conflict (be it in the form of External or Internal Conflict) is to make your character want something worth acting for. The thing that this character wants is his goal.

There are different types of goals in a story. There are the character's initial conscious goals and the character's end conscious goals (each of these are things he knowingly wants, either at the beginning or end of the story). These are external goals.

Then there are your character's subconscious goals—the ones stemming from his subconscious needs (internal goals). This is usually referred to as the character's *story goal* because it is the goal that you, the writer, have in store for him at the end of the story. Sometimes it may be a *secret wish*, something he longs for but fights or doesn't think he can have. (Note: just as one can have subconscious goals, one can work subconsciously to get them, too. Moreover, people can subconsciously act to defeat themselves and preserve their internal conflict). Nevertheless, to be well-formed, a character needs both external and internal goals that intertwine.

Finally, there are also the character's individual scene goals, the smaller goals he sets for himself in order to get his internal or external goals At this point, however, don't focus on scene goals. We'll discuss those when we get to...you got it, scenes.

Okay, so in order to create action-inducing conflict, let's start with the easiest type of goal, the character's conscious, external goal. This external goal needs to be a specific, tangible and concrete goal so the reader and the character can clearly know if and when he has achieved it. The external goal focuses the action and keeps the story moving forward, even if the goal changes or the character's plans to achieve the goal change. In fact, if the character is going to change throughout the story (and we already know we want this Character Arc), then it makes sense that his external goal is going to change, too.

As the character acts to get his external story goal and the conflict he encounters escalates, he will respond to the conflict (prompting more action), and his external goal should change or his plan to achieve his external story goal should change (prompting yet more action).

So, why do we need to add an internal subconscious goal (that the character isn't initially aware of but the reader is)? Because it's a vehicle for showing maximum character growth.

It's human nature to: 1) be complacent and not take risks; and 2) go after something only when forced and, even then, to choose the easiest and safest thing to obtain. We try to avoid going after the things we need most because often they are also the things we fear most. We'll only acknowledge and go after them when pressed.

Let's expand on this.

An internal goal/subconscious need is often based on the character's greatest fear, a belief system he or she has taken on about the world. False beliefs usually develop from a character's back story/shadow and often affect the way a person presents himself to others. Screenwriter Michael Hague refers to a false belief about the world as an *Incorrect Core Belief*, which makes person act out of *Identity* (a mask) rather than *Essence* (his true self). Ironically, a character's Incorrect Core Belief also drives the character's actions through Internal Conflict--he longs for the very thing he fears most, even if it's a subconscious longing. (You can show the reader the Internal Conflict even if the character isn't aware of it. This is what allows the reader to know the character is capable of changing.)

It makes sense, then, that your character is going to go after his most obvious goal first. He's going to go after that goal because something external in the plot (the Inciting Incident) forces him to act, not necessarily because the character knows something in his life needs fixing (remember, human beings are naturally complacent and resistant to change).

If your character was enlightened enough to go after his most basic, subconscious need at the beginning of the story, he wouldn't show much growth in the story, would he? Nor would he draw readers in and make them root for his success. The story journey is what makes him face his fear and go after what he really needs. Put more concisely, if the story begins with the character wanting a concrete, external goal and you want to show the character changed, then the story should naturally end with him wanting a different goal. Usually, this turns out to be the character's subconscious, internal goal (whether manifested by an external object or not), i.e., his *story goal*.

To summarize so far, let's work backward:

You have a character who gets his goal at the end of your story (this is his story goal or subconscious internal goal, which satisfies his subconscious needs, but can also be manifested by an external object).

This goal is likely not the same goal he started the story with (this was his concrete external goal).

The reason his goal changed is because he encountered action-inducing conflict that made him change his goal or modify his plan for getting his goal. This caused him to grow as a person.

From the beginning of the story, the reader suspected your character had the capacity to change and was willing to see that change because there was something the reader liked about your character or found relatable.

The fact that your character gets his goal (the goal that gives him what you, the writer, knows he really needs) satisfies the reader's expectations and answers your Story Question.

The fact that your character is better off for having obtained this goal rather than his original goal should once again prove your Theme.

EXAMPLE:

In Virna's paranormal romantic suspense series, she created a world in which Humans had warred with Otherkborn (non-human creatures including vampires, weres, and felines). Vampires are immortal but essentially wasting away due to a vaccine the U.S. created during the war. In effect, the vaccine changes the properties of human blood so that it can no longer nourish vampires.

In the first book, the hero is the leader of the largest vamp clan in the United States. His conscious external goal at the beginning of the story is to marry a female vampire in order to insure the survival of his race.

When he is offered the chance to lead an F.B.I. team made up of Otherborn and go after the vampire antidote, this puts him in close proximity with the heroine, a human. As a result of conflict he encounters, his immediate goal changes. In addition to finding the antidote, his goal becomes to keep the heroine close to him and insure her sexual surrender. However, he still plans to marry a vampire. At the end of the story, as a result of the escalating conflict he's encountered, his goal has become to marry the human female, something that requires balancing his duty to his people with his own desires. This is because his subconscious, internal goal (his story goal) is to find true love and happiness.

The events in the story and the ending of the book prove Virna's Theme: In order to live a fulfilled life, one must balance duty with desire. The story Theme justifies the answer to the Story Question: yes, the hero defeats the antagonist in order to get his goal — the love of the heroine — but only because he learns to balance duty with desire. And, of course, he ends up saving his clan, too!

THE IMPORTANCE OF A HIGH STAKES, PERSONAL MOTIVATION IN DEVELOPING CONFLICT

Now that you know what types of goals your characters will have, how do you formulate the specific goals and show their development? In addition, how do you make it believable that the character will act to get his goal?

To get to the core of your character's goals, Jennifer Crusie suggests you ask yourself what the character wants (this is usually the external conscious goal at the beginning), then what the character really wants (the modified goals in the middle of the story), then what the character really, really wants (the internal goal/possibly manifested by the external goal at the end of the story). Reveal these goals to the reader slowly so she can see it, start analyzing why the character is doing certain things, and start rooting for him or her to get what she really needs.

Likewise, give the character a realistic and compelling "motivation" to achieve his goals. Characters should be motivated by something visceral, emotional, and urgent (otherwise it would be too easy for them to give up the goal).

You also need to establish urgency. It won't help your pacing if your character's need isn't immediate. Ask yourself why your character needs his goal, when he needs it, and why something else won't work. If the character needs money, what does he need it for and why so soon?

Try to establish some kind of dire consequence if the character does not get his goal. This is called *stakes*. The higher the stakes, the more urgent the goal, and the more likely the character will act, sometimes unpredictably and unreasonably (i.e., out of character for him and his usual fears), to get his goal.

Make your goal personal to your character. Think of reasons why it has to be him or her going after the goal instead of someone else.

At some point, the actual goal becomes less important than a character's growth in trying to achieve the goal. You create high stakes and make the conflict personal by making sure something the protagonist *and* the antagonist feels an attachment to and cares for is on the line. The stronger you make the conflict, the more hell you put your character through, the more significant the character's triumph will be and the more intense the reader's feeling of catharsis will be experienced.

So now you can see why, in the "10 For 10" triangle, conflict is listed above goal, and motivation, right? Because you need both these things to create effective conflict, which is needed to create action, answer the Story Question and prove your Theme. In sum, to make powerful conflict, ask yourself:

- What does the protagonist want? Really? Really, Really?

- What is his/her motivation?

- Why can't (s)he have it?

- Why can't (s)he walk away from the problem or let someone else handle it?

- What's at stake if (s)he doesn't get it?

EXAMPLES: CREATING CONFLICT THAT'S PERSONAL & UPS THE STAKES:

The hero is a cop trying to track down a particular suspect; the heroine believes the suspect is innocent

- This is a conflict in beliefs but the hero and heroine are not truly in conflict until one of them acts to impede the other in order to achieve a specific goal. Ideally, each of them will cause conflict for the other.

The hero is a cop attempting to take a suspect into custody; the heroine believes the suspect is innocent and tries to convince the cop of this fact.

- This is External Conflict so long as the heroine, in trying to convince him the suspect is innocent, is stopping him from taking the suspect into custody.

The hero is a cop trying to track down a particular suspect; the heroine believes the suspect is innocent and takes action in order to prevent the cop from catching the suspect. (Example: lies about where he is, physically restrains the cop, etc.)

- This is stronger External Conflict because the heroine is

actually doing something active to prevent the hero from taking the suspect into custody.

The hero is a cop trying to track down a particular suspect; although the evidence points to the suspect, the hero's gut instinct tells him the man is being framed or he's had prior experiences with the man that indicate he has good character.

- This is the hero's Internal Conflict.

The hero is a cop trying to track down a particular suspect; the heroine believes the suspect is innocent. However, although the heroine believes the suspect is innocent, she once advocated for someone else's innocence and helped that person get away with something, only to find out she was wrong.

- This is the heroine's Internal Conflict.

The hero isn't sure he'll ever be as good a cop as his father, who was tough-as nails and never wavered in his decisions; the heroine believes, based on prior relationships, that men can't be flexible or change.

- This is Internal Conflict that might lead the hero and heroine to take different actions than the previous Internal Conflicts

The hero's last girlfriend was a "true believer" defense attorney who was killed by one of her clients; he's certain that the heroine's naïve thinking is going to get her killed and doesn't want that kind of heartache. The heroine's father was domineering and unfaithful to her mother; she's certain the hero is narrow-minded and therefore exactly like her father (his failure to consider the suspect's innocence reinforces this belief) and she's sworn never to get involved with such a man.

- This is romantic conflict based on Internal Conflict and External Conflict. It will keep them apart romantically and create sexual tension.

The hero is a cop trying to track down a particular suspect who killed his best friend; the heroine believes the suspect, her brother, is innocent.

- This makes it personal.

The hero is a cop trying to track down a particular suspect who killed his best friend and has threatened to kill a victim every 24 hours; the heroine believes the suspect, her brother, is innocent.

- This makes it personal and raises the stakes.

The hero is a cop trying to track down a particular suspect who killed his best friend and has threatened to kill a victim every 24 hours and is now targeting the heroine; the heroine believes the suspect, her brother, is innocent.

- This makes it personal and raises the stakes even more.

EXERCISE:

1) Develop the goal and motivation for your protagonist and antagonist. Example: The antagonist wants revenge against the man who killed his mistress, so he's determined to kill this man's lover, the heroine's sister.

2) List five types of characters that could actively help your protagonist achieve his/her goal. Likewise, list five characters that could help the other antagonist prevent the sympathetic character (protagonist) from getting his/her goal. Example: *Characters who can help the woman save her sister: cops, sister's best friend, sister's mother, sister's boyfriend, or sister's friend. Characters who can help the husband get revenge/kill the woman's sister: hired help, a friend, a lover, a high-ranking city official, someone who betrays the cop.*

You May Be A Romance Writer If...

- You and your critique partners subconsciously use different variations of each other's character's names.
- You buy your friends books "just because," but you probably don't read most of them.
- You cry when your writing partner moves to another state.
- Your family is used to you "checking out" at odd times and making a mad dash for your computer.
- Your friends constantly elbow your husband and ask if your book is based on reality.
- You realize you've finally met a group of people who "get" you.
- You often start conversations with your husband by saying, "So what do you think of this idea...."
- You know who your true friends are because they ask you what you're writing or how's it going rather than whether you've finally published.
- You've become an expert at "running contests" where the prize is your book or something with your brand.
- You daydream about the perfect pen name and where it would alphabetically place you on a bookshelf.

CHAPTER 10

BREAKING DOWN PLOT WITH THE THREE ACT STRUCTURE

Did you know? The Three Act Structure highlights the specific and identifiable events that make up your plot.

As discussed above, the plot of your story is really the character's story journey and how he is forced to adapt to conflict through action and change. Once you have a grip on character, conflict, and plot, you can start writing (as many "pantzers" do), think about specific story structure then start writing (probably still considered "pantzing"), or organize and outline your story ahead of time (something that "plotters" do to varying degrees of detail) as you utilize a specific story structure.

Although there are many forms of story structure, romance writers have commonly relied upon Joseph Campbell's mythic story structure based on The Hero's Journey. Essentially, the hero's journey begins with a protagonist who gets a "call to adventure," initially resists, is forced to accept the call, encounters several obstacles along the way and gets various kinds of help, faces his demons, prevails, then returns to his Ordinary World and makes that world better as a result of his journey.

Many romance writers are also drawn to the Three Act Structure, a structure based on escalating tension and one used by screenwriters, including Michael Hague, Alexandra Sokoloff, and the late Blake Snyder. Successful romance writers who use the Three Act Structure are Lori Wilde, Susan Meier, and Nina Bruhns. To some degree, it appears that Jennifer Crusie and Bob Mayer use the same principals, though they have been condensed.

Does this necessarily mean you *need* to know Three Act Structure? Of course not. But again, why not learn what it's about? While a story might successfully defy all traditional notions of story structure, such a story is only unique in comparison to what has come before it. Furthermore, the writing process is fluid and often amorphous, which makes it both exciting and scary, especially when you are first starting out. Story structure provides a starting point that can foster creativity in a "controlled environment" or can be used as a "safety net" to explore other options.

The Three Act Structure breaks "Story" into acts, stages, and Turning Points, all representing different phases of story progression and Character Arc. In particular, Three Act Structure represents a story's progression through escalating conflict, which is designed to pose the central Story Question: Will the protagonist defeat the antagonist and get what he wants?

Three Act Structure provides not only an outline, but guidelines for building conflict and keeping track of pacing.

Act I deals with set up and the problem facing your main characters.

Act II deals with the increasing complications that occur when your characters try to deal with the problem.

Act III plays on the raised stakes that have gotten so high that the antagonist and protagonist must finally face off. It contains the crisis (*Black Moment*) and *Climax* of the story, and it is at the Climax where the story-building tension erupts and then free falls, giving the reader catharsis.

Virna truly didn't understand Three Act Structure until she attended the Low Country RWA Master Retreat in South Carolina. There, Susan Meier explained the correlation between a character's Internal Conflict and External Conflict. She then gave a workshop on synopsis, and Virna realized that her method of summarizing Romantic Conflict tracked the Internal and External Conflict structures she'd been discussing earlier. And finally, when Nina Bruhns broke down the concept of Character Arc so that it also tracked the Three Act Structure, things suddenly became much clearer. Because Virna had never seen all these principles tied together visually, and because Virna was so excited that they might actually work that way, she started plotting them out.

Yes, many writers rely on the Three Act Structure, but some also have narrowed or expanded upon it. The key is finding a framework that works for you. A particular framework might work better during different stages of the writing process.

For example, both Bob Mayer and Jennifer Crusie describe narrative structure in a narrower way than Michael Hague, but the bottom line is that their descriptions fit within the broader category.

Bob Mayer identifies five key points to narrative structure:

- INCITING INCIDENT
- ESCALATING COMPLICATIONS
- CRISIS
- CLIMAX
- RESOLUTION

You could take these key points and start brainstorming plot points. Or, you can decide to use a slightly more detailed structure to brainstorm.

For example, you can use the eight key points identified by Jennifer Crusie in her essay, *Stalking The Wild Editor: How To Get Published, Maybe*.

- Inciting Incident: TROUBLE STARTS
- Act One: PROTAGONIST MAKES PLAN
- First Turning Point: UP THE CONFLICT

- Act Two: PROTAGONIST CHANGES PLAN
- Second Turning Point: POINT OF NO RETURN
- Act Three: PROTAGONIST STRUGGLES
- Third Turning Point: PROTAGONIST SEEMS TO LOSE
- Act Four: PROTAGONIST FIGHTS ON
- Climax: TROUBLE ENDS

As you will see, Bob Mayer and Jennifer Crusie define narrative structure in a different way, but every component they rely on is also in the Three Act Structure. The Three Act Structure simply expands upon them, providing, depending on your outlook, more detailed guidance or more things to worry about. Also, note that both Bob Mayer and Jennifer Crusie start the narrative structure at the Inciting Incident—that is, the time the trouble starts and the situation that sets up the protagonist's external goal.

Jennifer Crusie strongly believes that this is the way to hook the reader. The story starts with the problem because that is the basis for the central Story Question—the conflict between the protagonist and the antagonist. The story ends when the problem is solved; that is, after the central Story Question is answered.[10]

Other people believe that establishing the character's Ordinary World, as advocated by the Three Act Structure, allows the writer to establish the reasons why the Inciting Incident is going to drive the character toward certain actions. For example, in their Break Into Fiction® plotting workshop, Mary Buckham and Dianna Love start their Break Into Fiction® method of plotting with the Everyday World. This is the method they prefer because, as the Break Into Fiction®: 11 Steps to Building a Story that Sells book

---

[10]   For this reason, it is well-known that Crusie is vehemently opposed to prologues. She considers them back story that the writer should assume the reader knows, or else should reveal in small bits throughout the story.

clarifies, the Everyday World provides a reference point for the reader to see the overall change and contrast in the protagonist's character by the end of the story, after the series of story events have impacted and created character growth. However, as Mary also warns, providing a set-up needs to be as tight and relevant as possible. And the story still needs to start with a strong hook that makes the reader want to read more. Thus, if a prologue is used, it needs to be compelling and not just a tool for dumping in back story (commonly called an "information dump" or "back story dump").

Three Act Structure tracks Story like this (Turning Points are indicated by parenthesis):

ACT I

- STAGE 1: SET UP/VIEW INTO THE PROTAGONIST'S ORDINARY WORLD
- Turing Point 1: (OPPORTUNITY FORCES CHARACTER INTO ACTION AND STARTS CONFLICT)
- STAGE 2: PROGRESS
- Turning Point 2: (SOMETHING UNEXPECTED HAPPENS, LIKELY THE FIRST DEFEAT, RESULTS IN CHANGE OF PLANS OR GOAL)

ACT II

- STAGE 3: INCREASED COMPLICATIONS
- Turing Point 3: (GREATER SETBACK RESULTS IN CHARACTER'S FULL COMMITMENT AND TO POINT OF NO RETURN)
- STAGE 4: FINAL PUSH; PROTAGONIST APPEARS TO BE LOSING
- Turning Point 4: (MAJOR SET BACK THAT RESULTS IN THE BLACK MOMENT)

ACT III

- STAGE 5: REALIZATION/AFTERMATH
- Turning Point 5: (CLIMAX)
- STAGE 6: RESOLUTION

EXERCISE: Using the protagonist you created above, describe what his/her Ordinary World looks like before the story opens.

CHAPTER 11

TURNING POINTS

*Did you know? Turning Points are the major events in your plot
that take the story in an unexpected direction.*

According to the Three Act Structure, Story is broken down
into three distinct acts, with two stages (distinct narrative
components that make up an act) separated by one Turning Point
in each act, and with one Turning Point separating each act. The
structure is useful because it tells us what "should be" happening
to our characters at certain parts of the story in order to build
conflict, and force the characters and the reader towards the
Climax.

ACT I				ACT II				ACT III		
STAGE 1	TP 1	STAGE 2	TP 2	STAGE 3	MID; TP 3	STAGE 4	TP 4	STAGE 5	TP 5	STAGE 6

Turning Points are an essential element of the structure and
serve a very important purpose. Turning Points are what keep
the reader interested in your book because they *redirect* the
plot/character's action and promote character development.
Turning Points hold up the sagging middle of your story.

Jennifer Crusie describes Turning Points as "mini-climaxes."
She also explains that story can be visualized as a clothesline, with
a beginning and an ending, but a middle that sags the more
laundry you hang on it. However, if you are able to stabilize that

middle at certain points, the whole laundry line will be kept taut and will be able to support more of what you place on it.

Mary Buckham and Dianna Love describe Turning Points as "twist points." They "twist" the character into taking an action and, due to that action being taken, the protagonist will be changed from that point forward. The twist points create "the catalyst for character growth" because at each point, the character has the chance to turn back, but doesn't. Instead, he acts, which affects change and growth. With every new twist point, it will be harder for that growth to unravel at the end when the character is faced with the Black Moment or Climax. As each of the twist points occur, there is more to lose for the protagonist because of the growth that has happened.[11]

TP 1: The first Turning Point is the one that takes the character from his Ordinary World. It is the Inciting Incident that forces the character to act in a way he normally wouldn't have.

As the character focuses on getting his external goals, outside forces start to promote change in him. With this change, the character will start to slowly reveal who he is, only to face a new conflict.

TP 2: In Turning Point two, the conflict escalates and something unexpected happens that drives the character to modify his goal or plan, as well as reveal even more about himself.

TP 3: The *Midpoint* (the twist in the story that comes in the middle of the book, or at Turning Point three) is the point in the story where the character's decision not to walk away changes everything. This is the "point of no return." It is the 180-degree turn that takes the character on a new route. It is through his response to this change that the greatest growth will occur, but the change will not be complete. His resolve to change completely will be tested one more time.

---

[11] Note that Mary and Dianne identify three twist points, but Three Act Structure incorporates five Turning Points.

TP 4: Conflict is at its highest at Turning Point four (the Black Moment). At this moment, the character's worst fears come true and he retreats back behind his mask (Identity) for a time. However, because the character has been strengthened by his story journey, he actually learns something from the Black Moment and comes to some greater realization. This realization allows him to face his greatest fear in an external way (the Climax). As a result, the character sheds his wounds and Incorrect Core Beliefs forever and wins his happy ending.

TP 5: As indicated above, the Climax is the Turning Point where the antagonist and protagonist are both on the page and only one can win. It has been the author's destination all along. Its purpose is to cement the change that the protagonist has been making thus far, and to insure his final transformation. The Climax often mirrors the opening scene in some way in order to provide an image of how the protagonist and his world has changed from the beginning of the book.

The acts, stages, and Turning Points of the Three Act Structure can also be used to literally track the pacing of your story. Susan Meier clued Virna in on this trick and it made the concept of story structure have practical application to her manuscript in a very specific way. Keeping track of how many pages you have devoted to a particular act, stage, or Turning Point can keep your book from being unduly heavy or sparse in any one area.

ACT 1				ACT 2				ACT 3		
STAGE 1	TP1	STAGE 2	TP 2	STAGE 3	MID; TP 3	STAGE 4	TP 4	STAGE 5	TP 5	STAGE 6
pp. 1-30		pp. 30--130		pp. 131-231		pp. 232-332		pp. 333-374		-end

Since Virna writes single title romantic suspense and paranormal romantic suspense, she shoots for approximately

100,000 words per manuscript, which is around 400 pages. Based on what each stage and Turning Point is supposed to accomplish, Susan Meier pointed out that most pages are going to fall within Stages 2, 3, and 4. This is the meat of your story and also the most difficult to write. These stages will be roughly the same number of pages (100 pages for a single title). The reason the Midpoint occurs at approximately page 230 rather than page 200 is because of the "set up" beforehand and because of the build up to the Inciting Incident. You can also structure your story so that fewer pages are used at each stage after the Midpoint, reflecting that pace has picked up and everything is hurtling towards the story Climax.

Keeping track of page numbers allows you to track pacing and whether you are spending too much time or too many pages on any one stage in the story. If Virna writes her story and spends 200 pages in Stage 3, she knows she's off track and that she's not leaving herself enough room for the second half of the book. In addition, if her Midpoint event occurs in the story at page 325 (which it actually did when she first charted out her story with Susan Meier), then she knows it comes far too late in the story. She can then make adjustments as she writes, not when she's written the whole thing so that she then has to rip it apart, a painful process to be sure.

Remember, these are all guidelines, but you're free to do whatever you need to do for your story. Depending on whether you are writing single title or category, you can modify the page designations. Use the page numbers to track how much time you should be spending where, when certain events are occurring, and whether you are writing too much when the pace needs to be quickened.

EXERCISE: Answer these questions based on what you started in the previous exercise.

    1. Based on where your character starts out, what could be the 180-degree change that occurs in the Midpoint?

2. What is the worst thing that could happen to your character in the Black Moment?

You May Be A Romance Writer If...

- You're constantly asking yourself whether promotion really makes a difference.
- Most of the people you'd like to meet live in New York.
- You know how it feels to be thrilled for someone and jealous of her success at the exact same time.
- You want people all over the world to recognize your name while at the same time you want to fade into the background.
- You've experienced the worst insecurity and depression of your life because of writing but you still want to keep doing it.
- You think you'll never write anything better than the story you just wrote.
- You madly check Amazon for a good review and then are surprised when a bad one ruins the entire day.
- You believe in happily ever afters.
- You're overwhelmed. *Extremely* overwhelmed. But you wouldn't want to do anything else.
- You have other creative interests, such as scrap booking, photography, dance, etc

CHAPTER 12

RAISED STAKES & DIMINISHED OPTIONS LEAD TO TRANSFORMATION/CHARACTER ARC

Did you know? Conflict causes your characters to act and grow, which ultimately results in Character Arc?

As discussed, Turning Points keep the reader intrigued by changing the direction of the story. Each detour is deliberately designed to drive the protagonist and the reader towards the Climax and stems not only from raised stakes (upping what the character has to lose), but by the diminished options available to the protagonist, and then by the characters' actions and the consequences of these actions. The raised stakes start at the Inciting Incident and continue through the Black Moment (the moment the protagonist realizes his worst fear has come true), where it leaves the protagonist with two choices: be destroyed or be transformed.

Raised stakes, however, do not occur solely in the exterior plot. They are reflected in External Plot Conflict, Internal Character Conflict, Romantic Conflict, and Character Arc. Accordingly, each of these types of conflict has its *own arc* in the story that tracks the protagonist's character growth. It is by facing all three layers of conflict that the protagonist is able to grow and face the antagonist in the climax.

Now, you might be asking yourself why we didn't talk about these conflict arcs in the "Conflict" section. However, by talking about them here, we're emphasizing the fact that the conflicts are trackable as mirrors of "progressive complications." That is, when looked at closely, the purpose the three conflicts is to raise the stakes and escalate the conflict in order to drive action. This progression of conflict is subsumed under the concepts of Plot, Three Act Structure, and Turning Points.

EXTERNAL PLOT CONFLICT

Probably the most readily accessible type of conflict is External Plot Conflict. This is the conflict that is happening on the page and on the screen. It is the external events that are happening to the protagonist and antagonist (hopefully because of each other) and, in turn, the things they do as a result of these events. It is the push-pull, forward-backward, action-reaction sequence that takes us from the character's Ordinary World and propels her to the Climax and Resolution.

In the External Conflict portion of the Three Act Structure, the protagonist starts in his/her Ordinary World, and usually has some kind of external goal based on his/her back story. Then, something important (the Inciting Incident) pushes her to change her goal. This something important is usually something connected with the antagonist. This makes sense, because as soon as the protagonist acts to get her new goal, the antagonist is also going to have to act in opposition to her. Conflict with the antagonist will pull the protagonist away from her goal. As a result, she realizes she must modify the plan to get the goal, or change her goal completely. This type of movement toward a goal, opposition to achieving the goal, and modification of plan or goal, continues and escalates throughout the book, with complications getting worse and worse. Finally, the stakes are raised so high that the protagonist and antagonist face off during the Climax.

EXERCISE: Brainstorm several, escalating ways that the antagonist is going to actively get in the way of your protagonist getting his/her goal. *Example: The hero wants to catch a murderer. The heroine wants to live. The antagonist, the heroine's husband, is sending his goons after the heroine to kill her. Then he comes after her himself.*

INTERNAL CHARACTER CONFLICT

According to Susan Meier, Internal Conflict is the heart of the romance novel. As we've alluded to earlier, Internal Conflict is often evident in the formation of an Incorrect Core Belief, a broad and general conclusion about life formed either from a character's shadow/back story or a specific experience. These beliefs can be based on something they saw in childhood, experienced themselves, or even know about another person.

For example, a hero who was neglected by his emotionally distant mother may form the Incorrect Core Belief that any woman who wants a career would be a selfish, uncaring mother. A heroine who was repeatedly cheated on may form the Incorrect Core Belief that entertainers are incapable of being faithful. The broader a belief is, the harder it is to break down, because in some ways it can be proven true. According to the teachings of screenwriter Michael Hague, a person acting out of an Incorrect Core Belief is said to be acting out of Identity because he is presenting a mask to the world.

In the Internal Conflict portion of the Three Act Structure, characters initially act out of Identity. In acting out of Identity, they usually confirm each other's Incorrect Core Beliefs. However, as the exterior plot progresses and the characters are forced to act (and change), they begin to reveal more and more of their true selves (Essence). When they get scared, they retreat behind their masks. And the process repeats itself. As such, scenes should reflect the breakdown of your characters' Incorrect Core Beliefs, but also their backsliding.

Usually by Turning Point three (the Midpoint), the main characters have released most of their Identity at some cost to themselves. The Black Moment is the worst thing that can happen externally, but also internally because it confirms the Incorrect Core Belief that the character had at the beginning of the story. At the Black Moment, the character scampers back into Identity. Soon thereafter, the protagonist faces her biggest realization.

Once she accepts that realization and acts, she completes the Character Arc that will allow her to defeat the antagonist and become her true self.

EXERCISE: Brainstorm several ways that your protagonist acts to hide who he really is from people in general (try to stay away from focusing on the love interest) (i.e., jokes around a lot or doesn't say much of anything).   Then brainstorm how he'll start to show more of who he really is (i.e., reveal meaningful things about his past or dreams).   Think of something that could happen to make the protagonist pull back and retreat behind his mask again.

ROMANTIC CONFLICT BETWEEN HERO & HEROINE

Just as the Inciting Incident forces the protagonist from his Ordinary World to start the external plot, some catalyst (either the Inciting Incident or something else) is going to bring the hero and heroine together.   In the best Romantic Conflict, the hero and heroine each have formed Incorrect Core Beliefs and when they act in Identity at the beginning, their Incorrect Core Beliefs will rub against each other.   Moreover, the hero and heroine may have opposing goals, which will be the basis for External Plot Conflict but cause even greater Romantic Conflict.

Susan Meier gave this example: the hero and heroine meet at the hospital after the heroine accidentally runs her car into the hero's sister.   The hero has formed an Incorrect Core Belief that loyalty to family is the most important sign of one's ability to love.   The heroine has formerly formed an Incorrect Core Belief that no one will ever accept her for who she is, flaws and all.   The hero's need to support and protect his sister is automatically going to rub against the heroine's need for forgiveness, especially when he acts in Identity by criticizing or blaming her, maybe even yelling at her.

Likewise, perhaps they discover that the heroine is the woman trying to close the resort that has been in the hero's family for generations.   He views her as having no sense of family loyalty, thus no ability to love, but in reality she has been ordered by her controlling mother to shut down the resort and feels complying is the only way to earn her mother's love. Now, her goal and actions in Identity are conflicting directly with his external goal and Incorrect Core Belief.

Slowly, because the hero and heroine must stay together for some reason, they will cautiously get to know one another and reveal their true natures. One reason they may have to stay together is because one has a need the other can fulfill. For example, in the above scenario, the hero has to stop the heroine from closing down the resort. Maybe the hero is a cop who can protect the heroine from a man who has been stalking her.

The hero and heroine will reveal their Essences through actions, internal narrative, and dialogue (even dialogue from other characters who know them better). Their Essences must give the reader reasons to root for the hero and heroine. It is through seeing their Essences that the hero and heroine will start to fall in love with each other, but at the same time, the more Essence they reveal, the more vulnerable they become. To protect themselves, they will move back and forth between Identity and Essence. There has to be a good reason why the hero and heroine continue to stay together. Then, something compelling separates them. This is the Black Moment.

The Black Moment in the External Conflict should coincide close in time to the Black Moment in the Romantic Conflict. Hurt in Essence, the hero or heroine scampers back into Identity. The wound has to be so bad that they *think* they won't be able to recover. Something has to happen (some action or some piece of information revealed) to change that, something so significant that the hero goes after the heroine, or the heroine goes after the hero. They may not resolve the Romantic Conflict until after the External Conflict is resolved, but in the end they accept that they will risk staying in Essence, thus risk being hurt, for love.

Notice how the Romantic Conflict and External Plot Conflict co-exist. They balance and interweave, so that one is challenged and nurtured because of the other. The characters cannot achieve their external goal without growing in the relationship, and they cannot grow in the relationship without learning from the External Conflict.

EXERCISE: Repeat the previous exercise, but his time focus on how the protagonist reveals and hides who he is from his romantic interest.

INDIVIDUAL CHARACTER GROWTH (CHARACTER ARC)

Character Arc essentially tracks the back and forth nature of each of the above conflicts but focuses on how the conflicts force the character to change as a whole. It looks directly at what is "wrong" with the character's Ordinary World at the beginning of the story and how he slowly begins to make changes to correct these wrongs. Major change occurs at the Midpoint, but it is not a complete change. Complete change does not come until after the Black Moment, when the character must make a "do or die" decision to be the person he truly can be, or else forever go back to the way things were. And, of course, in order to defeat the antagonist and get his happy ever after, the only thing the protagonist can do is face his demons completely.

Let's look at these concepts more closely by focusing on the protagonist and the antagonist, and the type of change they will undergo during the story.

WHO IS THE PROTAGONIST AND WHAT DOES HE/SHE HAVE TO LEARN?

As discussed in the "Character" section above, the protagonist is the character that is trying to achieve something in your story, and the person who grows and changes the most because of the events of the story.

From the moment trouble begins, story plot is going to focus on what is wrong with or missing from the protagonist's life and how he goes about fixing it (with well-motivated goals). The protagonist's action in trying to achieve his goal drives him forward. Almost always, the protagonist will abandon the goal he had at the beginning of the story because as he grows and changes throughout the story, so do his goals. Opportunities for reflection, decision, action, and growth by the protagonist are provided throughout the story by plot Turning Points, which turn the character in another direction and keep the reader off balance.

WHO IS THE ANTAGONIST AND WHAT DOES HE/SHE WANT?

The antagonist forces the protagonist into action towards a particular goal (usually not in a positive way), but then the antagonist continues to act in order to prevent the protagonist from getting what he wants. This forces the protagonist to act some more, and to modify his goals or plan. This then causes the antagonist problems, so he adapts and acts. And so on. And so on.

This is your plot.

It is this constant push and pull throughout the story that keeps the reader wondering what happens next and forms the basis for the story's central Story Question: can the protagonist defeat the antagonist to achieve his/her goal? (If we keep repeating this, it's because it's such an important question to remember!) This Central Story Question drives both your characters and plot in the story. In romance, it is this "drive" the reader savors.

An antagonist, like the protagonist, must have flaws and virtues, and must be well-motivated to achieve his goal. Otherwise, he/she could appear to be a caricature.

At the beginning of the story, the antagonist should be stronger (whether physically, in circumstance, or in what he's willing to do) than the protagonist. However, the reader has to know it's going to be a fair fight, if only the protagonist steps up to the plate and is willing to change. Why? Think about it — the reader wants your protagonist to work for his happily ever after, but it's got to be a fair fight. If your antagonist is weak, then the reader is going to assume the protagonist's "win" will be easy, and the reader has less motivation to find out how he wins. Likewise, if your antagonist is so strong that the protagonist seems weak, the reader may lose respect for your protagonist or his ultimate victory may feel unrealistic. In both cases, the reader makes assumptions that cause him to lose focus interest in the story.   What you want is to create a likeable protagonist and worthy antagonist so that the reader forgets the happy ending waiting at the end and only cares about how the protagonist is going to react or adjust when repeatedly confronted with the conflict caused by the antagonist.

Character reveals plot and conflict, and plot (*specifically how a character acts in response to opportunity or disaster*) reveals a character's *inner character*. Layered characters don't always make the best decisions at first, but many learn to do so as time and opportunity continues.

Towards the end of the book, your protagonist will pull ahead of the antagonist, but only after having done some heavy-duty soul-searching and work. This is where all that character growth comes in.

Remember how your character has been slowly reacting and growing and changing his goals in response to conflict? He's been revealing more and more of his true Essence as he gradually overcomes his fears? Well, all that conflict escalates until it must reach a peak, forcing the character to face the thing he absolutely fears the most.

At this point, the reader knows on some level that the protagonist is going to triumph in the Climax. The point of the romance story, and of the protagonist's journey through it, is that *if he had been faced with the climactic situation at the beginning of the story, he wouldn't have won.* The story lends credibility and significance to the protagonist's win/happy ending because by that point he has earned it. All his previous steps in the journey, all the conflict and action and readjustment, have caused him to grow and learn (this is the protagonist's Character Arc), leaving the reader satisfied.

At the same time, however, note that the antagonist (in general and assuming the antagonist is not the hero or heroine or otherwise redeemable character) does not have a Character Arc. The antagonist's needs will not be met. His situation will not be fixed. He wants something and is willing to do a lot to get it, but because he is not willing to or unable to change or grow in the same way that the protagonist is, he is not going to end up getting what he ultimately wants. He is, in effect, destroyed.

Now, what if the antagonist is the hero or heroine? This is not a classic protagonist/antagonist relationship, where the antagonist is defeated. However, the hero and heroine are still protagonist and antagonist because they should, at the very least, always be in romantic conflict. In addition, they can have actual External Conflict: what one is doing to achieve his goal makes it more difficult for the other to get what he wants, and vice versa.

With a hero/heroine--antagonist/protagonist combination, the protagonist will still be "the winner." She will get her ultimate story goal, and the antagonist will not. However, because the hero/heroine are together at the end, the antagonist cannot be "harmed" in his defeat. In fact, his defeat must have met his needs in some way that his original goal could not have. The antagonist will realize the value of his defeat because he will have experienced his own Character Arc/growth throughout the story, unlike traditional/villain antagonists.

PULLING IT ALL TOGETHER; THE FOUR "Cs" INHERENT TO ANY ROMANCE:

Now we want to show you some charts we created that clearly delineate the four "Cs" of any romance novel (Conflict [External, Internal & Romantic] & Character Growth [Character Arc]) and how they all complement and track one another through the three acts in the Three Act Structure.

ACT I:

- STAGE 1: SET UP
- TP 1: (OPPORTUNITY FORCES CHARACTER INTO ACTION AND STARTS CONFLICT)
- STAGE 2: PROGRESS
- TP 2: (SOMETHING UNEXPECTED HAPPENS, LIKELY THE FIRST DEFEAT, RESULTS IN CHANGE OF PLANS OR GOAL)

THREE ACT STRUCTURE ACT I (from Set Up/Ordinary World to Opportunity to Progress to First Defeat/Change Of Plans)	
CONFLICT	
Internal: Protagonist vs. Self/Past	The protagonist presents herself in a certain way to hide who she really is. The antagonist and love interest push her to reveal her true self. She provides glimpses, but her Internal Conflict (based on her back story) makes her pull back before revealing too much.
External: Protagonist vs. External Antagonist	The protagonist has a goal before the Inciting Incident. This initial goal is based on her back story. The Inciting Incident pushes her to change her goal. Conflict with the antagonist pulls her away

	from her goal. As a result, she realizes she must modify her plan and acts accordingly.
Romantic: Protagonist vs. Hero/ine (Love)	The protagonist and hero meet. Sexual attraction pushes them toward each other, but conflict (clue: consider two boxes above) pulls them away from each other. At the same time, however, something compelling (not just attraction) keeps them together.
Character Arc: Protagonist vs Ordinary World (Complacency)	Things in the protagonist's life need fixing, whether she admits it or not. In encountering conflict towards her goal, she has some realization and 1) acknowledges something in her life isn't helping her attain her goal; and 2) acts (pushes) to change this. Eventually, however, her Ordinary World/complacency pulls her back.

ACT II:

- STAGE 3: INCREASED COMPLICATIONS
- TP 3: (GREATER SETBACK RESULTS IN CHARACTER'S FULL COMMITMENT AND TO POINT OF NO RETURN)
- STAGE 4: FINAL PUSH; PROTAGONIST APPEARS TO BE LOSING
- TP 4: (MAJOR SET BACK THAT RESULTS IN THE BLACK MOMENT)

THREE ACT STRUCTURE	
ACT II (from Increased Complications to Greater Set Back/Point Of No Return to Final Push to Major Set Back/Black Moment)	
CONFLICT	
Internal: Protagonist vs. Self/Past	The protagonist shows more and more of who she really is, but vacillates. At the black moment, when he believes his fears and need to hide behind a mask were warranted, he will retreat behind that mask.
External: Protagonist vs. External Antagonist	The protagonist has a new plan to achieve her goal. Conflict with the antagonist (Raise the stakes!) pulls her away from her goal. She fully commits to getting her goal (Raise the stakes!) and her actions make it

	impossible to turn away from it. Afterwards, however, the antagonist ups the conflict until the protagonist suffers a major set back (things seem lost)
Romantic: Protagonist vs. Hero/ine (Love)	The protagonist begins to open up emotionally to her love interest as she realizes her love/feelings for him. However, close to the time of the external plot's black moment, something happens in the romantic relationship that makes the protagonist feel betrayed and makes her pull away from the hero.
Character Arc: Protagonist vs Ordinary World (Complacency)	Same, except the protagonist is meeting greater and greater resistance to her achieving her goal (Raised Stakes!) When the worst thing happens both in the external plot and the romantic relationship, the protagonist retreats back into her shell.

ACT III:

- STAGE 5: REALIZATION/AFTERMATH
- TP 5: (CLIMAX)

THREE ACT STRUCTURE	
ACT III (from Realization/Aftermath to Climax to Resolution)	
CONFLICT	
Internal: Protagonist vs. Self/Past	The protagonist comes to some realization that shows why she can permanently give up her mask and be the person she's been trying to be. Her willingness to grow earns her a HEA.
External: Protagonist vs. External Antagonist	The protagonist comes to some realization that allows her to face off with the antagonist and defeat him in the climax. Her life is changed for the better.
Romantic: Protagonist vs. Hero/ine (Love)	When the hero and heroine are apart, the protagonist realizes why she retreated and becomes willing to risk all for love. Her willingness to take risks earns her a HEA.
Character Arc: Protagonist vs Ordinary World (Complacency)	Each time the protagonist acts to achieve her goal, she is met with resistance. At this point, it appears the antagonist is going to win. All looks lost until the protagonist makes a huge

By Virna DePaul with Tawny Weber

	realization and acts, reflecting she can change permanently. Because of her journey, the protagonist and her world are changed for the better and she earns her HEA.

You May Be A Romance Writer If...

- Your kids ask you whether you love your computer more than you love them.
- Sometimes you love and hate your job with equal passion.
- You think you're never going to be good enough.
- You think you're a genius one day and an idiot the next.
- You sit in bookstores as people walk by and try to avoid looking at you.
- You look forward to copy and galley edits.
- You experiment with plotting methods.
- You know what a blog tour is.
- You've tried a magic bulldozer.
- You know your brand, platform, and hook.

CHAPTER 13

RAISING THE STAKES IN EVERY SCENE WITH SCENE AND SEQUEL

Did you know? Your characters should experience conflict (at a minimum) in every scene.

Just as a story has a structure that guides the protagonist and the reader toward the Climax and Resolution (the end of the story that shows how the protagonist's world has been transformed), individual scenes also have a structure that serves that same purpose. Knowing about this structure before you even start brainstorming will help you craft scenes with narrative drive, which means you might have less to revise.

Chapters are comprised of *scenes* or *sequels*. Virna first learned this from Lori Wilde, who learned about it from Dwight Swain's book *Techniques Of The Selling Writer*. This is one of those concepts Virna now sees everywhere, but at the time had no idea it existed.

A scene is a unit of time where a reader "sees" an action or event occurs. It is usually grounded by place or time or the point of view of the character who actually observes the action. A scene should be in the POV of the character that has the most to lose in the scene. Every Scene should have its own protagonist and antagonist.

A sequel is often not distinguished from a scene, but a writer should know the difference. A sequel looks like a scene, but it serves a different purpose and has different components. Technically, it serves the same purpose as a sequel to a movie, which continues the narrative of a pre-existing movie. In this case, it continues the narrative of a previous scene. It is less active and more ruminative than a scene. It is not a scene because it does not involve a character with a specific scene goal nor does it end with a disaster. You want to use a sequel when you want a character to reflect on the previous scene.

A novel will have far more scenes then sequels, since scenes reflect the actions characters take in order to achieve their goals, as well as the conflict they encounter.

Scene or sequel breaks indicate either a switch in character POV or a break in time or place. Either before, during, or after writing a scene, you need to make sure you have a purpose to the scene, that you've picked the right POV character to reveal the scene, and that you've set the scene for the reader.

PURPOSE

A scene must advance the plot. It should reveal clues or character, add suspense or raise tension, or provide conflict. No scene should serve the same purpose as another. If it does, try to combine the scenes. The more purposes a scene serves, the better. When the purpose of your scene is accomplished, the scene is over.

POV

Writers are taught not to switch POVs in a scene (what is often called "head hopping" because the reader "views" the scene from one character's perspective and then another's within the same scene). Yes, it can be done, but it can confuse the reader. In addition, it can create problems when trying to formulate scene "disasters" as will be explained below.

SETTING

Finally, set the scene to orient the reader. Do it quickly. Make sure that within the first paragraph, the reader knows the "when, who, and where" of the scene. Setting is mood and it can also reveal different things about your character. The setting can even be a character in the sense that it can actively help or work against the character. Now, let's expand on the differences between scene and sequel.

SCENE

The components of a scene are Goal; Motivation; Conflict; Disaster.

A character's scene goal is simply something he or she plans to do as a step toward achieving his or her exterior goal. Try and make the scene goal, like the exterior conscious goal, concrete and immediate.

In addition, ask why the POV character needs to accomplish his goal today and not yesterday or tomorrow? This establishes well-developed motivation.

Likewise, something needs to be preventing the POV character from achieving his/her scene goal. The conflict can be interior, exterior or both. The best kind of conflict is active conflict between two characters. You can label scenes "character x versus character y" to make sure there is this type of conflict.

Finally, reveal how the POV character's action in trying to achieve his goal results in *disaster*, something that, whether he achieved his goal or not by the end of the scene, makes the POV character realize the situation is a little worse.

By creating a disaster in every scene, you raise the stakes and diminish the character's options, something that is necessary to achieve transformation. You also leave the reader wanting to know what's going to happen next.

The disaster doesn't have to be a catastrophe and it doesn't have to turn things in a different direction the way a Turning Point would (although it can), it just has to make things worse for the character than they were at the beginning of the scene. This is true whether he achieves the scene goal or not. The disaster can simply be that the character learns additional information that ups the stakes, even if it is the character's internal/emotional stakes. Moreover, the disaster is the POV character's disaster — something he knows about; it is not the disaster that is "off the page" and that the author, but not the character, knows is coming. The scene disaster cannot happen outside the POV character's understanding. She has to realize things are worse. Why? Because this gives her another goal to pursue (one that's connected to something that has happened before) or makes him change his plans to achieve the same goal in his next POV scene.

This is how you escalate the stakes and how you keep the momentum between one scene and the next. If you incorporate more than one POV into a scene, finish out the "GMCD" with the disaster affecting the first POV character, even if you are still in the POV of another character.

To insure you do this correctly, answer the question whether the POV character got his/her scene goal or not. The answer must begin with a "yes but..." or a "no and furthermore..." Then, in the character's next POV scene, try to base his/her scene goal on the previous scene disaster.

In summary, a scene should have the following components: purpose, correct POV character, a sense of who, when, where to orient the reader, and answer the questions:

1. What is the POV character's scene goal?

2. What is his motivation?

3. What is the Internal and/or External Conflict getting in the way of the scene goal?

4. Did the POV character get his goal? "Yes, but" OR "No, and furthermore."

Finally, remember how you want to prove your Theme in every scene? You do this proactively, by showing how your Theme is true (for example, in my story, that the hero got his happy ever after only when he was able to balance duty with desire). You can also show the opposite of your Theme to prove it. For instance, if your Theme is "letting go of the past leads to love," you can show that holding onto the past leads to two characters breaking off an engagement. In *Chosen By Blood*, Virna proved her theme (one must balance duty with desire) in a scene when the hero blindly chose duty over his desire to be faithful to the heroine--he ended up hurting her and driving her away for several years.

EXERCISE: Based on the questions you've answered above, brainstorm a scene that incorporates the elements of goal, motivation, conflict and disaster. Then, brainstorm another scene in the same character's POV that is based on the disaster in the previous scene.

SEQUEL

The components of a sequel are: emotion from the POV character (regarding what happened in the previous scene); quandary (about what he/she should do next); decision (a decision made after mulling over the quandary); and action (action taken in regard to the decision made).

The action that the character takes in a sequel will lead him into his next POV scene. Just like the disaster in a scene, the action insures narrative drive and momentum between sequels and scenes so that the sequel serves an actual purpose.

EXERCISE: Based on the two scenes you brainstormed above, brainstorm a sequel that is based on the POV of the other characters in the above scenes.

CHAPTER 14

ANSWERING THE STORY QUESTION OF WHETHER THE PROTAGONIST ACHIEVED/EARNED HIS GOAL/HAPPY ENDING

Did you know? The way your book ends answers your Story Question and proves your Theme?

In the "10 For 10" triangle, the final element of Story is actually answering the Story Question—does the protagonist defeat the antagonist and achieve his story goal? However, simply because a romance requires a happy ending, and the hero and heroine are together at the end of the story, does not mean that the protagonist achieved his or her initial external goal.

Remember, the protagonist can achieve an external goal, but he doesn't have to. Sometimes, a happy ending requires that the protagonist fail to get his external goal completely and instead get something better. In most cases, he will have realized in the course of the story that his original goal wasn't what he really wanted- i.e., not in alignment with his internal need, which he will recognize is more valuable.

Whether or not he gets his external goal, however, the point is that, in order to fully satisfy the reader, the story does not stop at the end of the Climax, when the protagonist defeats the antagonist. Just as setting up the Ordinary World in the beginning gives us something to measure the character's flaws and needs by, showing the final impact of the protagonist's journey gives us something to measure his transformation by.

How will the three conflicts we discussed above ultimately impact the resolution of your book? Let's take a look.

STAGE 6: RESOLUTION

THREE ACT STRUCTURE ACT III (RESOLUTION)	
CONFLICT	
Internal: Protagonist vs. Self/Past	The character FULLY reveals who she is and WINS.
External: Protagonist vs. External Antagonist	The protagonist faces off with the antagonist and WINS.
Romantic: Protagonist vs. Hero/ine (Love)	The character RISKS ALL for love and WINS
Character Arc: Protagonist vs Ordinary World (Complacency)	The protagonist's life is changed for the better.

The reason your protagonist is able to achieve his happy ending is because he changed enough in the story to earn it, but more importantly his change proved your Theme true. For example, it was because Virna's protagonist in *Chosen By Blood* learned to balance duty with desire that he was able to save his clan and win over the heroine.

EXERCISE:

1. Think of how you want your character to be different at the end of the story than he/she was at the beginning. Think about how this can be manifested both by beliefs

but also behavior, how she dresses, the world she lives in, etc.

2. With respect to your antagonist, how has his failure to grow resulted in his defeat? How has his failure to adopt your thematic assertion defeated him?

CHAPTER 15
LOVE IN TRANSLATION[12]:
MAKE YOUR STORY YOUR OWN

STEP 3: BRAINSTORM
CHARACTER, BACK STORY AND PLOT POINTS

"There is only one success…to be able to spend your life in your own way." *--Christopher Morley, Author*

Now that you are familiar with some of the crucial components of Story, do you have a plot you're working on? Or maybe you simply have a story idea in your head? Or an idea for a character that you'd love to flesh out? Either way, you're at a great point for brainstorming before you start writing again.

According to Diane Pershing, there are three things a writer should focus on before she begins writing:

1. The main characters and what drives them
2. The Inciting Incident of the story
3. The general story arc of the characters that includes several key plot points, surprises, Turning Points, and Resolution.

---

[12]   Love In Translation by Wendy Tokunaga

These points are consistent with the way Virna usually plots her books. With regard to some of the first few books she wrote, here's what Virna has to say:

I started my first manuscript with an idea for a character: a tightly-wound ambitious female prosecutor with a hidden, dark past that made the hero, a laid-back, charming defense attorney, the worst possible person for her. Based on this general character sketch, I asked myself what would be the Inciting Incident of the story — the thing that would take her from her Ordinary World and force her into the event of the story. I decided the best thing to do was bring her past into her present in a way that was sure to get her attention — in the form of a criminal defendant, a former friend with personal knowledge of her dark side. From there, I asked myself what would be the obstacles along her journey and how the hero could help or hinder her along the way. Accordingly, I was able to see the arc of the story, which would take her from uptight, wounded, and stuck in the past to open, trusting, and ready to move on with her future.

With my third manuscript, I started not with a character sketch but with a plot idea — a young girl gets in a fight with her mother about an older boy she has a crush on; she runs away, only to return and find her mother has been murdered by a homeless man she had previously befriended.

Based on this plot idea, I then brainstormed characters. What kind of girl would this situation be the hardest for? In my opinion, it was a girl whose relationship with her mother had always been close but had recently been damaged by her parents' divorce, which she blamed on her mother.

In addition, I thought about who would be the worst hero for this character? How about the boy she and her mother had fought over, and the same man who now wants to reopen the investigation of her mother's murder, thus forcing her to relive her grief and guilt all over again?

With these characters and general plot points, it was much easier to then think about twists and turns and story arc. The heroine would start out mistrusting the hero, but then would start to trust him. What would make her mistrust him again? Keeping a secret from her? Threatening another relationship that is important to her? How about if he begins to suspect that her father, the only parent she has left, was the one who actually murdered her mother?

As you can see, the couples I created in both manuscripts, as well as the ensuing plot points I brainstormed, were designed to challenge my character based on what very little I knew about them. Both heroines happened to have dark pasts and excess guilt they were running from. The surest way to create conflict and strong emotion, then, was to make them face that past and guilt at the onset of the story.

When you begin brainstorming characters and plots points, keep these tips in mind:

- Brainstorm the details that will help you show your reader who your characters are and why they deserve their win or defeat at the end.

- Do this for your main characters including the hero, heroine, and antagonist if different.

- Start at the character's "beginning" and work forward to the present where you can, but know that much of the character's back story will likely keep developing as your story progresses. An alternate to this is to start with the characters Internal Conflict--what emotionally drives them in this story, and work backward to understand how or why they hold this mistaken belief.

- Know that the character's past/back story is going to help form his/her goal at the very beginning of the story. Then, circumstances (Inciting Incident) as well as Internal Conflict/motivation (affected inevitably by back story and/or physical events and the character's

Incorrect Core Beliefs), will cause him to rethink this goal and make decisions that will forever affect the course of the story.

- Explore the sequence of each main character's goals and actions. Remember, a motivated goal causes character x to act, but we know that the other characters' actions in trying to get their goals cause character x's conflict. When encountered with this conflict, character x must make a decision (either to keep the same goal but adjust his plan or change his goal), then act. How he acts is going to create conflict for the other characters. This pattern will continue simultaneously for the protagonist and the antagonist, with the antagonist gaining ground until after the Midpoint, at which time the protagonist is forever changed and begins, through his actions, to gain ground so that he can win in the Climax.

CHAPTER 16
IN TOO DEEP[13]: MAKE SURE YOU'RE NOT

STEP 4: CONFIRM YOUR STORY FITS THE SUBGENRE/LINE YOU'RE TARGETING

I find the great thing in this world is not so much where we stand as in what direction we're moving." --Oliver Wendall Holmes

Although this step may seem like backtracking, you might find that after brainstorming, the story you intended to write is not the one you've outlined. It might be darker than you intended. Or it might be more complicated, with several subplots that won't work in a category romance that requires a shorter page count. As such, take a quick moment to confirm whether your story fits the subgenre you are targeting. Remember that reader expectation is not only formed with respect to genre and subgenre, but individual imprints within publishing houses and individual lines of category romance. Again, the best way to know what distinguishes one imprint from another is to read the books.

SUBGENRES OF ROMANCE

---

[13]   *In Too Deep* by Tori Carrington

- CHICK LIT: Humorous, sometimes snarky-toned novel that often focuses on young women entering the adult, professional world for the first time. No happy ending is required and the subject matter can be light or weighty. A chick lit mystery usually involves a crime-solving heroine with attitude.

- COMEDY: Romance with a light, humorous tone.

- CONTEMPORARY: Romance set in the present time where the hero and heroine live in a modern world that most readers can easily relate to.

- EROTICA: Focuses heavily on the sexual relationships between the characters. Erotica usually pushes sexual boundaries with topics such as multiple partners and kinky situations.

- FANTASY: Imaginative fiction involving magic and adventure in a setting other than the real world

- HISTORICAL: Romances set in historical times.

- INSPIRATIONAL: Inspirational romances celebrate traditional Christian values, although they can focus on other faiths.

- LITERARY FICTION: Fiction that is designed to be thought-provoking and leave a deeper impression. It is not necessarily designed to leave the reader with an optimistic feeling about the world. Usually, the language is formal, the imagery is lush and the characters complex.

- MYSTERY: In a mystery, a crime has already been committed at the beginning and the question is who committed it and why.

- MYSTERY (COZY): A cozy mystery is one in which an ordinary person (amateur sleuth) is trying to solve a crime. There is usually no graphic violence, profanity, or explicit sex.

- PARANORMAL: Paranormal means a phenomena outside the range of the normal. Paranormal romance is often about creatures of another kind/species/race operating in the normal world, whether humans are aware of their existence or not. Some typical paranormal creatures include werewolves, fairies, vampires, or witches.

- ROMANTICA: As defined by Romance Writers of America's (RWA) special interest chapter, Passionate Ink, erotic romance is about the development of a romantic relationship through sexual interaction. A happily ever after is required as in with any romance, but the sexual content is more explicit.

- SCIENCE FICTION: A novel with imaginary elements that are largely possible within scientific theories. Largely based on writing "rationally" about alternative possibilities, although many elements may require suspending disbelief as well.

- SUSPENSE: Suspense leads up to a big event or dramatic moment with tension being a primary emotion. This tension is usually one source of the conflict in the story. A mystery is going to have rising tension, too. However, in a romantic suspense, a crime may have occurred at the beginning, but another crime is going to occur. The main thread is trying to prevent the next crime, rather than simply finding out who committed a previous one. It's usually restricted to one town or local area, with only a limited segment of the population at risk.

- THRILLER: A thriller is a story with a quick pace, lots of action, suspense and plot twists. Usually there's a ticking clock that keeps the reader on the edge of his seat, wondering who is going to win, the good or bad guy. (Note: There can be a ticking clock, such as a serial killer's deadline, in a suspense, too.) A thriller is often a race against time to prevent a disaster that will affect a large population — an entire country, a continent, or the world.

- URBAN FANTASY: Fantastic elements are incorporated into a modern-day, urban setting. Often protagonists must navigate a fantasy world that coexists with the "real world," and includes elements of magic, or magical/paranormal creatures such as werewolves, fairies, vampires, or witches. Usually, female protagonists struggle to come to terms with their powers and world.

- WOMEN'S FICTION: A story that centers on a woman or primarily women's issues, not necessarily the woman's romantic relationship. Does not require a happy ending.

- YOUNG ADULT: Stories that are written for young adults and project the voice of the young adult from the point of view of a young adult. Deals with Themes that are current and interest the young reader of today, even if the story is set in historical times.

CATEGORY VERSUS SINGLE TITLE

Category romances are shorter books (around 50,000 to 70,000 words) that are typically part of serial imprints, with each series focused on a particular type of book (sexy, funny, family, suspense, etc). Note that category romance is distributed like a magazine, with a regular number of books being issued at regular times of the month. Category romances are guaranteed to be sold to bookstores and they are sold all over the world. Regular readers pick up category books with clear expectations of what they will be reading.

Most category romances are published by Harlequin Enterprises under the Harlequin or Silhouette lines. Typically because of their shorter length, category books often do not incorporate subplots. The plot focuses on the hero and heroine. According to Susan Meier, in category, the External Conflict can be resolved half way through the book, leaving the emotional conflict for the second half. There is sometimes a five-page "rule" in category where typically the hero and heroine can't be apart for more than five pages, and they have to think about each other for no less than every two to three pages.

Harlequin, Silhouette and Mills & Boon are divided into "lines," with each line falling into its own category. Passion, Home and Hearth, Suspense, etc. Each line has a specific "reader promise." For example, Blaze promises a sexy read with a strong, contemporary heroine. SuperRomance promises an emotional journey with conflicts typical of today's women.

In contrast, a single title book is not published as part of a publisher's series category line. It is longer and focuses on more than just the external plot (and romantic relationship) between the hero and heroine. The novels often have secondary characters and subplots, and the External, Internal, and Romantic Conflict typically runs to the end of the book. Although single titles may be written as a series, each book stands alone in packaging. Single title books are usually around 100,000 words long.

CHAPTER 17

AS YOU DESIRE[14]:
GETTING YOUR BIG MESSAGE ACROSS

STEP 5: EXPAND UPON YOUR STORY'S THEME; BRAINSTORM MOTIF AND SYMBOLS

"Art washes away from the soul the dust of everyday life."

--Pablo Picasso

THEME

Hopefully you already came up with a thematic message for your story when you were brainstorming and filling out your outline. If not, think of it now. Remember, it's the big message assertion that you want to make. The lesson of the story, if you will. Got it? Now, confirm your Theme by diluting it to its most basic form.

The following exercise was taught to Virna by Lori Wilde and is designed to make you think about what your book is really about, give you the practice to easily articulate it, and thread your Theme throughout your work in progress. Virna's also found it helpful as a jumping off point for brainstorming scenes.

1. Try to encapsulate your Theme with a one-word verb. For example, in one of Virna's manuscripts, her Theme was: In order to be happy, a person has to accept their

---

14   *As You Desire* by Connie Brockway

past mistakes, forgive themselves, and move forward. As such, the one word that encapsulates her Theme was: Acceptance.

2. Try to encapsulate the opposite of your Theme with a one-word verb. For example, what is the opposite of acceptance? Rejection.

3. On one side of paper, write down the first word: acceptance. On the other write the second word: rejection.

4. As fast as you can, write down fifty things that signify or relate to your first word. It can be specific to your characters or it can be a universal symbol of acceptance. For example, for acceptance: a mother's hug, sorority sister, the song Black and White by Acceptance. If you run out of steam, list words that are similar to accept/acceptance (receive, tolerate, understand).

5. Next, as fast as you can, write down fifty things that signify or bring to mind the second word. For example, for rejection: a shove, closed eyes, crossed arms, cold shoulder.

6. As you write your story, try to keep this list handy. It will help you prove your Theme in every scene you write by showing the existence and effect of certain elements. You can also plant subconscious clues about your Theme by incorporating one of these Theme words/phrases in your scene. The word you choose can depend on how you are proving your Theme in that scene — proactively or by opposites.

MOTIF

A motif is a recurring element in your story that represents a subject, Theme or idea. The purpose of a motif is to support or establish the mood of your story. It creates a visual or other sensory pattern that provides "background" meaning. For example, for a woman who has lost all hope of having children, the motif might be barrenness or emptiness. Visual images to represent this motif could be a dry creek, an empty glass, a bald head, or a mouth devoid of teeth. Subconsciously, the more times you use this motif, even when you're not expressly reminding your reader of the character's barrenness, your reader might think of it.

SYMBOLS

A symbol is something that represents another thing. A symbol can be an object or a gesture. It can be song or weather condition. A symbol encompasses not just a representation of some thing, but all the information we know about that thing.

There are universal symbols (those that are part of our "collective psyche" or culture) such as the cross or a peace sign or the scales of justice.

There are representational symbols (symbols that are used to give meaning beyond what is actually described). For example, in *Macbeth*, Shakespeare uses blood, both real and imagined, as a symbol for guilt. In addition, the raven is used as a symbol for ill fortune.

There are iconic symbols (symbols that are loaded with meaning in order to alert the viewer that something is going to happen). For example, if someone is killed whenever one of the characters drinks a glass of wine, drinking a glass of wine becomes an ionic symbol for death.

You can use symbols in your work and give them meaning by repeating them or giving them a bit of emphasis. In this way, you are deepening and layering the complexity of the elements in your story.

CHAPTER 18
WHERE DREAMS BEGIN[15]:
THE ESSENCE OF YOUR STORY

STEP 6: CREATE A TAGLINE, LOG LINE, STORY PREMISE AND HIGH CONCEPT PITCH IF POSSIBLE

"Bravery is the capacity to perform properly even when scared half to death." --General Omar Bradley

Now that you've thought about story structure and brainstormed your story and Theme, you need to be able to concisely state what your story is about. Why? Because whether you are talking to a friend, critique partner, instructor, agent or editor about your book, you want to be able to describe it quickly and thoroughly. This communicates that you know your story inside and out.

In addition, by creating short descriptions that speak to the heart of your story, you will have descriptive prompts to focus on during the writing process—they can remind you what you're really trying to write about. Note that while a one-word description (such as "acceptance") might help remind you of your main Theme, it usually isn't sufficient to describe what your book is "about," because it does not emphasize what makes your book special.

As Alexandra Sokoloff has said, "The time to know what your book is about is before you start it..."

---

[15]   *Where Dreams Begin* by Lisa Kleypas

No matter what your story is about, you should develop as many ways to describe it as possible. You can do this by coming up with a tagline, logline and story premise. Moreover, try to create a "high concept" pitch if you can. ("High concept" is a phrase often used more generically than it was originally intended; often "logline" and "high concept pitch" are used interchangeably). While you're at it, see if there's a way you can make your story high concept if it isn't already. Editors are always asking for the next "high concept" that makes your work stand out from others.

THE DIFFERENCE BETWEEN A TAGLINE, LOGLINE, HIGH CONCEPT, AND STORY PREMISE

A tagline is a catchphrase or slogan, especially one used in advertising. It gives the reader an immediate feeling or hook for your movie, but doesn't tell a whole lot about the story. There are some classic taglines out there:

Star Wars: In a galaxy far, far away…

Jaws: Don't Go Into The Water.

Aliens: In space, no one can hear you scream.

Then there are some newer ones. For example, the tagline for the new *A-Team* movie is: "There is no Plan B." The tagline for the movie *Law Abiding Citizen* with Gerard Butler is: "How do you stop a man from committing a crime when he's already in prison?"

A log line (what is sometimes called a "high concept pitch"), on the other hand, is a one-sentence description of the entire story. It does more than a tagline because it gives an idea of who the characters are (protagonist and antagonist), what the conflict is about, and what one can expect with respect to setting and/or mood.

According to Nina Bruhns, who learned about log lines from Blake Snyder, a log line should have the following components:

1. Convey the tone/mood/Theme of the book;
2. Convey a compelling mental picture that makes you sit up and take notice, usually by incorporating some kind of hook or surprise about the specific story
3. Convey main characters using somewhat conflicting adjectives, as well as reflect the dilemma of the characters
4. Convey a mental picture of scene/place

Alexandra Sokoloff gives the following example of a logline in her book, *Screenwriting Tricks For Authors*, about the movie, *Jaws*:

When a great white shark starts attacking beachgoers in a coastal town during high tourist season, a water-phobic Sheriff must assemble a team to hunt it down before he kills again.

Here's our version of a log line for the movie *Shawshank Redemption*:

Wrongfully convicted of his wife's murder, a soft-spoken accountant survives twenty years of abuse in prison and escapes still believing in the goodness of mankind.

In the above examples, you can see that the four elements defined by Nina Bruhns are met. In addition, all of them incorporate some kind of hook or surprise about the specific story. The "surprise" can be subtle (the Sheriff in Jaws is water-phobic; the man who survives twenty years of abuse in prison is a soft-spoken accountant), but the twist can also be more obvious (i.e., a Sheriff that is a serial killer).

What is high concept? High concept is a phrase coined from screenwriting. It is a blockbuster idea, one that has a hook and twist that is broadly appealing to a larger audience. According to Mary Buckham and Dianna Love, it's a film in which the director can cast any actor and have a "break out" film.

In simple terms, it's what every agent or editor is hoping will land on her desk—a story with the potential to be *big*. It's exact definition, however, is far more slippery and complicated.

A "high concept pitch" is similar to a log line. Although the high concept pitch doesn't have to encompass the main plot points of your book, it needs to provide the same type of emotional response one would get from reading the book. In this way, the log line and the high concept pitch are similar. However, to be truly "high concept" a pitch needs a special something that a log line lacks.

Lori Wilde describes a high concept pitch in her book, *Got High Concept? The Key To Dynamic Fiction That Sells*. Wilde indicates that a high concept pitch delivers five components in 25 words:

1. It's different;

2. It's universal;

3. It has instant emotional appeal;

4. You can immediately visualize the entire story; and

5. It can be stated in one sentence.

Alexandra Sokoloff makes a bigger distinction between a log line and a high concept pitch. According to Sokoloff, while a log line can describe an interesting story, she maintains it is not "high concept" unless "everyone who hears it can see exactly what the movie or book is—and a majority of people who hear it will want to see it or read it…"

For her, the ingredients of a high concept is one that has one or more of these things:

1. It's topical; about something that hits a nerve in society at the right time (i.e., cloning, sexual harassment)

2. It's universal (i.e., religion, dinosaurs, Christmas holidays)

3. It exploits a primal fear

4. It's about a situation most of us have experienced (blind date, father meeting a date, holidays with divorced parents)

5. It generates "water cooler talk" (affairs, illegitimacy)

6. It has a big twist (the main character who is really dead, the character who is a different sex)

No matter which method you choose, the point is that you need to be able to give a brief description of your book that is able to tell the listener what defines and distinguishes it.

But what about Story Premise? What is it?

A premise is defined as "an assertion or proposition that forms the basis for a fictional work." As you've learned above, you should have a thematic assertion in mind when you write, a global message that you want to convey to your reader. In our view (note that Alexandra Sokoloff uses premise and log line interchangeably), story premise restates your Theme but applies it directly to the hero and heroine's specific circumstances. In a way, it is a shorthand reminder of what role your hero and heroine serve in the story.

For example, if your Theme is that they only way to find true love is to let go of the past, then your heroine's premise may be: In order to find true love, the heroine must forgive her mother for abandoning her as a child and allow herself to be vulnerable with the hero.

BRAINSTORMING A BIG, HIGH CONCEPT, SAME BUT DIFFERENT STORY

Since we're talking about brainstorming log lines, premises, and "high concept" pitches, this is also a good time to discuss "high concept" stories in case you specifically want to brainstorm one of those.

We've already discussed the difference between a tagline and a pitch. A catchy tag line makes your audience take notice. A pitch describes what your story is about, adding depth and color, but doesn't give a whole lot of details. A Big Book, High Concept Same But Different Story is the successful execution of a high concept pitch.

A Big, High Concept, Same But Different Story should be:

1. Relatable
2. Recognizable
3. Twistable
4. Layerable
5. Expandable

Let's touch briefly on each of these subjects.

A story is relatable if it touches on a universal concept or Theme. In general, this concept is incorporated into the Theme of your story. Universal concepts are issues that have the greatest degree of meaning to the greatest number of people, which gives them mass appeal across time and cultures. They are intangible resources that almost everyone can relate to. They might also be described as "universal intangibles."

Not all people will agree on the meaning of or share the same perspective towards a universal concept, but all people will relate to the concept in some significant way. The way you tell your story tells the reader your position on a universal concept.

Some examples of universal concepts are: appearances, invincibility, sense of self, grief, trust, good vs. evil, redemption, justice.

Some examples of universal Themes (which focus on a specific aspect of a universal concept) are:

1. The redemptive quality of love
2. The transience of human life
3. The importance of companionship
4. The difficulties of living in a small/large town
5. The different stages of life
6. The uselessness/detrimental quality of life
7. The limitations caused by fear

Some examples of a thematic assertion (which makes an assertion about a specific aspect of a universal concept):

1. Only by facing our greatest fear can one truly experience the joy in life

2. Each phase of life is as important as the last

3. Isolation causes a person's worst qualities to intensify

4. A person's past matters less than his/her future

By hitting on a universal concept and Theme, you make it more likely a reader will be interested in what you have to say.

The same goes for making something in your story recognizable to your reader by incorporating a current issue/trend/icon. Doing this makes your work desirable to an already established group of people. (On the down side, given how long it takes to publish a book after a sale, trends can change, leaving you with something no one wants to read.)

Recent trends in romantic fiction have been: steam punk, paranormal, erotica, dark stories in general, dark Y.A., mash ups (ex: Pride & Prejudice & Zombies). Readers have also shown a desire to watch movies and read about medical romance, legal/forensic investigations, special ops/military stories.

Another key ingredient in crafting a "big book, high concept, same but different" story is adding an element of the unexpected, either because 1) Irony is created in that one element of the story exists in opposition to another; or 2) An element of the story is unique/has never/has rarely been done.

Take a current issue/trend and think how it can be turned on its head, happen differently, or go a different way. This garners interest because you exceed the reader's expectations. Of course, it also involves risk because you and the reader are taking a chance on something new, but it's a calculated risk. Recent twists in romantic fiction are:

1. Vampires and teens (Twilight series)
2. High lit and zombies (Pride & Prejudice & Zombies)
3. Native Americans/Shamans & Urban settings

In addition, what do you think of when you think of a "big book?" It's hard to pinpoint exactly, but we think it's accomplished when a writer imbues a high degree of complexity & sophistication to a written work. In other words, the writer layers the characters, the plot, the writing style, etc so there is the feeling of a lot going on without the reader feeling overwhelmed. Some ways that a writer is able to do this is:

1. Complex subplots and secondary plots
2. More secondary characters/relationships

3. Deeper emotions (bigger risks and stakes – something that impacts many in a major way)

4. Writing style – richer and more complex or evocative language; greater use of symbolism & motif

5. Larger Character Arc

6. Complex relationships/world

7. Things change constantly (more twists)

8. Major development of setting or setting used as another character

9. Bigger/more powerful villains/society

10. Deals with more points of view

11. Deals with different time lines

12. Involves a high degree of research/accuracy on a particular time period or subject

Moreover, agents, editors, and most importantly, readers are on the lookout for something that's going to stand apart from the crowd, but also something with longevity. That's why the Big Book, High Concept, Same But Different Novel should be expandable. This means that an individual story or book is capable of achieving continuing interest (i.e., series potential). Such continuity can be character-based, with characters that are colorful, interesting, and engaging, or in opposition to themselves, each other or preferably both. In addition, continuity can be more world-based, revolving around a world that raises intriguing social issues/conflicts.

Finally, we were on the fence about adding another ingredient to our list: Reasonable. We originally thought of this component as a way of discouraging the "out there" ideas but decided that was too limiting. What's too "out there" for one person might just be the "new, hot thing" for another.

So instead, just keep this mind: think about whether the details of the story are consistent with the mood, thematic message, trends and twists relied upon. Keep in mind that things must be fresh, but also that genre readers have needs and expectations that must be met.

For example, there's a definite difference between the following log lines:

Wrongfully convicted of his wife's murder, a soft-spoken accountant survives twenty years of abuse in prison and escapes still believing in the goodness of mankind

VERSUS

Wrongfully imprisoned for his wife's murder, a soft-spoken accountant discovers his passion for ballroom dancing and wins the prison's jitterbug competition

VERSUS

Wrongfully imprisoned for his wife's murder, a soft-spoken accountant launders money for aliens and ends up escaping to become the ruler of another planet.

What you write, however, is your decision. Don't let someone else's opinion sway you from writing what you want.

In addition, remember that there are plenty of stories that may not be "high concept" but are still compelling, sellable, and successful. The most important question is: does it grab and hold your attention? Is it relevant? Fresh? Sustainable? If you think in these terms, you increase your chances of a sale.

You May Be A Romance Writer If...

- You use the words "National," "pitch," and "Golden Heart" in the same sentence.
- You view summer as a "dead" time in the business.
- You know the difference between an Intrigue, Romantic Suspense, and Nocturne.
- You miss Ms. Snark but are grateful for Book Ends, Pub Rants, and the Waxman Blog.
- You know a Harlequin Hook might involve a baby, a cowboy or a pregnancy.
- You know the difference between erotica and romantica.
- You visit blogs like the Romance Bandits, Murder She Writes, or The Dark Salon.
- You squirrel away money for Brenda Novak's May auction for juvenile diabetes research.
- You can rattle off a log line as well as any screenwriter.
- You know the names of the acquiring editors at Pocket, Ballentine, St. Martins and Penguin.

CHAPTER 19

LOVER REVEALED[16]:

A BIGGER GLIMPSE INTO YOUR STORY

STEP 7: BRAINSTORM SCENES

"You are a child of the universe no less than the trees and the stars: you have a right to be here. And whether or not it is clear to you, no doubt the universe is unfolding as it should."

--Max Ehrmann

By now, you have brainstormed and struggled with structure enough to have a general idea of your characters and plot. You're clear on the tone and intent of your novel, where it fits within genre/imprint, and have nailed down different ways to describe your story. Now you want to start brainstorming specific scenes so you'll have more of a cohesive outline from which to write.

People do this several different ways. They jot down ideas on a piece of paper. They make plotting boards, with squares reserved for individual chapters or even scenes within chapters.

Virna tried both these methods, but didn't find them satisfying. For her, plotting boards are awkward, and she finds she can't fit enough information on post-it notes to really help her. Virna also finds trying to organize and reorganize the post-it notes isn't fun and that it's difficult to see an overall connection between one scene and the other. Virna much prefers typing notes into a blank word doc, in particular one that uses the

---

16   *Lover Revealed* by J.R. Ward

"Table" function to chart out the Three Act Structure, the four Cs discussed above, and various prodding questions. (We include examples of these charts in Part IV in case you find them useful, too.)

However, many people love plotting boards. Tawny, for example, uses a board and colored post-it notes to not only jot down scene ideas, but to track her storyline. With a different post-it color assigned to each vital area of the story (heroine's journey, hero's journey, romantic conflict, External Conflict, subplot) she is able to see all the threads and make sure they get enough page space and are all tied up neatly by the end of the story.

It's all about experimenting and finding a method that works for you.

Do some directed brainstorming of scenes based on the details you've fleshed out in Step 3, thinking specifically of Three Act Structure, and Scene and Sequel structure. Here are some ideas.

Create a scene that:

1. Shows your characters acting out a flaw

2. Shows your characters revealing their true nature, but reluctantly

3. Shows your character making some internal realization and modifying his goal or plan as a result

4. Shows your hero and heroine in romantic conflict

5. Shows your hero and heroine enjoying each other's company/flirting/having fun together

6. Gives the reader insight into the setting and the draw or challenges it poses for your characters

7. Shows interaction with secondary characters who in some way reveal something about your characters, their past, their current goal, motivation or conflict, foreshadow trouble, or act as a red herring

8. Introduces a new character or subplot

9. Develops a subplot

10. Shows the antagonist acting to cause conflict for your characters

11. Shows your characters reacting to trouble caused by the antagonist and adapting to overcome it

12. Foreshadows a bigger event to come

13. Is a flashback or reveals something in the character's past that has relevance now

14. Reveals something new about the antagonist to the protagonist

15. Reveals something the protagonist has been keeping a secret

16. Shows sexual tension between your hero and heroine

17. Shows your hero and heroine in an argument

18. Shows one of your characters in physical danger from the antagonist

19. Shows your character is feeling emotion but trying to hide it

20. Shows your character is alone and thinking to himself/herself

21. Shows your character meeting someone and instantly disliking/mistrusting him/her

22. Shows your character attempting to escape from a dangerous situation

23. Shows your character thinking about/revealing some kind of shadow in his or her past

24. Shows a sex scene between your hero and heroine

25. Shows someone from your character's past attempting to reconnect with him/her

26. Creates conflict or tension between your characters and the antagonist

27. Intensifies conflict or tension between your characters and the antagonist

Some general tips when brainstorming scenes:

Once you have a general idea for a scene, think about who the POV character is going to be. Then, focus on what that character's goal could be for the scene. Brainstorm motivation, conflict, and disaster. Also think about where the scene is set and whether this is the most effective use of setting for building conflict.

Remember when you are brainstorming scenes that if you include the disaster, the disaster will immediately develop the character's goal in his/her next POV scene. The scene ends when the purpose of the scene is achieved.

Concentrate on internal motivation as well as external. According to Mary Buckham, "emotion creates motivation and motivation drives action."

You will sometimes write "quasi-scenes" or "mini-scenes" in your story, called sequels. You can also try brainstorming some of these. Remember that a sequel shows a character reflecting on a previous scene, then taking or deciding to take some action. The elements of a sequel are: emotion, quandary, decision, and action.

Keep in mind ways to incorporate symbolism and motif, which will unify your story in a concrete way. Use your Theme list that you generated in Step 5.

Concentrate on setting and how it can enhance the purpose of your scene or how it provides an opportunity to show different sides of your characters.

Ask whether you have a ticking clock. Is there an internal or external clock that puts a limit as to how the character has to get his or her goal? This puts parameters not only on the story, but on the scenes.

CHAPTER 20
MY DEAREST ENEMY[17]:
BUT TRY TO WRITE A SYNOPSIS ANYWAY

STEP 8: WRITE A SYNOPSIS

"Some people wake up and dream of success, others get up and work for it." --Anonymous

A synopsis is a brief outline or general overview of your particular story's structure. It is a tool to sell a book that may or may not be written yet. Most writers hate to write it (and some editors hate to read them), but writing a good synopsis is generally crucial for submitting queries or manuscripts to agents and editors. It gives agents and editors a "summary" of your story's high points, as well as a flavor for your writing voice. Ideally, you want a synopsis to be both informative and entertaining.

Common criticisms of synopsis are they often become weighed down with too much detail or leave the reader with major plot questions. You do not want it to be an outline of every plot point in your book, or a summation of your character's back story or every action in the story. You do want it to reveal the major plot points of your book, *including* the ending.

There are many methods for writing a synopsis. There are just as many opinions on whether a synopsis is important or whether an agent or editor really wants to read them. One editor told

---

17   *My Dearest Enemy* by Connie Brockway

Virna she never reads the synopsis. On the other hand, many publishing professionals won't read sample pages unless the writer has shown she can write a good synopsis.

How long should a synopsis be? Ideally, anywhere from two to fifteen pages, but the length will generally depend on what kind of book you are writing, whether you are doing a lot of world-building in that book, and whether you are writing a series.

In particular, we like Susan Meier's method for writing a synopsis, which tracks the External, Internal and Romantic Conflict arcs discussed above. Here, we've modified Susan's bullet points to be more general and to comprise four distinct sections.

1. Establish the starting goal, motivation, and conflict of the hero and heroine (and possibly the antagonist), including the External Conflict. Establish what gets the hero and heroine together romantically, if different. Explain how their Incorrect Core Beliefs rub against each other. Explain what keeps them together anyway.

2. Next, show the development of the hero and heroine's romantic relationship even as the stakes of the external plot rise. Show the progression to the Midpoint, including their first kiss and how they slowly begin to reveal their secrets. Show what happens in the external plot to make the protagonist commit 100% at the Midpoint.

3. Next, show the escalating stakes in the External Conflict and how it causes the romantic conflict to break down. Show the hero and heroine revealing their true natures more and more, and how this increases their physical intimacy, as well.

4. Finally, show the protagonist's greatest fear come true, and how this causes her to pull away from the hero and retreat back into Identity (her mask/Incorrect Core Beliefs). Describe how she comes to some realization

that prompts her to face her greatest fear and show that her change/Character Arc is now permanent. Explain that, because of her willingness to change, she is able to face and defeat the antagonist, transform her life for the better, and get her happy ending.

You'll find an example of a synopsis using this method in Part II, when we break down Lori Wilde's book, You Only Love Twice. In addition, here are some other things to keep in mind about a synopsis:

- Leave out minor characters and minor plot twists
- Reveal what is at stake for major characters— what do they stand to lose?
- Do not leave cliffhangers or teasers—you need to show your reader how you are going to end the story.
- Think of it as a tool for augmenting a query letter or the hook.
- Consider giving your opening paragraph a hook or question. For example, "What if a woman finally takes a risk, only to have all her fears come true?"
- Make sure your hero and heroine are sympathetic, and that your antagonist's motivations are understandable to the reader.
- Try to portray external events, as well as romantic tension and emotion.

Now, you might be asking yourself how you would write such a detailed synopsis when you haven't even written the story yet. Of course, in this case, your synopsis is going to be more general, but it still has to be specific enough to show the reader that you can plot a book from the beginning to the end. It's also why this step comes after the one in which you try and brainstorm specific scenes.

Sometimes a writer gets the opportunity to submit a proposal to an agent or editor even though she hasn't completed the entire book. A proposal includes a synopsis, but only the first three chapters of the story. As such, a writer is well-served being able to write a synopsis without a complete manuscript. Whether you want to think of it as plotting or outlining or just being able to sell a great story idea in as many ways as possible, a synopsis is just another tool to add to your arsenal.

Once you've sold a few books, you'll often find your future sales being "on synopsis" rather than on a completed story, as well. By mastering this skill early, it'll make those later contracts much easier to achieve.

CHAPTER 21
ALL THROUGH THE NIGHT[18]:
MAKE TIME FOR IT

STEP 9: WRITE AND REVISE

"A decision is more than a wish. When you decide to get something done, it will get done. When you truly decide, it is more than just a vague intention. It is more than saying you are going to do it. It is more than hoping to get it done someday. It is a commitment that you make to yourself. When you truly decide, it will happen." --Ralph Marston

What do you do once you've done all the steps above? You do what you *really* want to do. You let your muse take over. You write, write, write, whatever this process may involve for you.

We've heard of people who will only write forward because going back and editing what they've written (before they've got a rough first draft) impedes their forward momentum too much. Other people prefer to review what they've written and revise it before beginning a new writing session. Still other people have been known to write with their monitor covered so they aren't distracted by the screen and tempted to "fix" what's on it.

The most important thing is to get your story down.

Then you revise.

Then you write some more.

---

18   *All Through The Night* by Suzanne Forster

In particular, when you revise, it sometimes helps if you know what to look for. Yes, you're looking for grammar mistakes and typos, but revisions are about so much more than that. Alexandra Sokoloff, for example, does a specific read-through for suspense elements. In addition, the Break Into Fiction® method of plotting by Mary Buckham and Dianna Love gives tips on how to improve pacing and characterization by using simple steps in their book for revising.

To help you focus on making your manuscript as compelling and polished as possible, here's what we recommend you keep in mind while writing your manuscript and/or look for during revisions:

YOUR BEGINNING:

- Does your opening set the right mood for the entire book?

- Can your reader readily identify who the protagonist is? If he/she is flawed, have you shown he/she is redeemable?

- Does your story open with the protagonist in conflict with the antagonist or someone linked to the antagonist?

- Is your antagonist realistic/sympathetic/well-motivated?

- Have you described the initiating event and why it had to happen now as opposed to any other time?

- Does the reader know the problem to be solved within the first ten pages? The first twenty?

YOUR MIDDLE:

- Have you escalated the conflict and stakes between your protagonist and antagonist?

- Has the increased conflict or stakes resulted in a significant (but incomplete) character change for your protagonist?
- Have the events of the story taken unexpected turns?

YOUR CLIMAX:

- Is it a fight or flight situation?
- Are the protagonist and antagonist engaged in a battle, on the page, in which the protagonist is victorious?
- Have you shown how your protagonist has grown so that he/she can now defeat the antagonist, when he/she wouldn't have been able to at the beginning of the story?
- Have you closed all sub-plots before the climax?

YOUR ENDING:

- Does the resolution result in an emotional payoff for the reader?
- Will your reader believe the protagonist has worked for the happy ending?
- Is the protagonist's world transformed for the better?

PAGE BY PAGE:

- Do you have any back story dumps? Sprinkle back story information throughout your story in small bits, on a need-to-know basis.
- Do you remain in the correct POV and is the POV clear to the reader?
- Are you "showing not telling" what your characters experience? Are you describing their tactile sensations

(feeling, taste, and hearing, not just sight) so the reader can experience what they are?

- Do you use lots of strong nouns and verbs, and avoid adverbs (-ly words), which are weak verbs?

- Do you use a balance of narrative and dialogue? Dialogue can reveal character, advance plot, or provide expository information, but having too much dialogue will make it hard to establish emotion and deep thinking with your characters.

- Do you have any "as you know" language? — This is a sign of back story dump or repetitive information.

- Are you hiding critical information from the reader that will make them mad? Readers need to know what is happening or they may become frustrated. Suspense is tension, not surprise or confusion. Filter information subtly.

- Do you employ the rule of three (repeat clues three times, repeat the beginning of sentences three times to create impact)?

- Do you make clear who is speaking while using dialogue tags sparingly? You don't need to mention names unless clarifying who is speaking. Also, when there are only a man and a woman in the scene, he/she works nicely.

- Do you create tension by having a character's actions go against what they say/believe?

- Can you cut down on expert details that will confuse the reader (i.e., medical or legal details) while still providing flavor and realism?

- Do you put conflict on every page, even if Internal Conflict?

- Can you have action rather than dialogue by having a person meet someone in person rather than on the phone? Show important conversations on the page w/ characters face to face.

- Do you vary sentence structure and length? Ex: look at the number of paragraphs you start with someone's name.

- Try cutting out the word "that" even when used correctly. It's usually unnecessary and amounts to a nounal conjunctive.

- Don't over-explain, which slows pace and dialogue. You don't need to say "He held the book in his hands." "Held" implies he is using his hands.

- Do you write the stimulus before the response? Don't describe a character's reaction before the reader knows what they are reacting to.

SCENE BY SCENE:

- Do you set the scene early so your reader knows where the action is taking place? Does the setting evoke emotion in the reader? Can it? Can it take place in a more interesting setting?

- Is the scene told from the most effective POV character?

- Does your scene have a purpose (move the plot forward or reveal new information or reveal character)? If not, you don't need it. Consider combining scenes.

- Have you started the scene as far into the action as possible?

- Can you label every scene as "one character versus another character or thing" to insure you have built-in conflict?

- Have you supported your thematic assertion in every scene?

- Do your scenes incorporate goal, motivation, conflict and disaster (ending on something provocative that shows how things are now worse/more complicated than they were before)?

- Does the action in the scene evoke an emotional response?

- Does the scene focus on one unit of time or jump around?

- Does the scene end so as to raise a question in the mind of the reader?

- Have you woven subtext in the scene?

- Have you shown emotion through dialogue, thoughts, biological response/feeling, or through some kind of action?

AS A WHOLE:

- Do you show you trust your reader by not over-explaining or repeating information?

- Have you shown arcs for your characters' internal, external and romantic conflicts?

- Do your major characters have Character Arc? If not, why? If so, how are they different at the end than the beginning?

- Does the protagonist's Character Arc support your thematic assertion?

- Do you have Turning Points that turn the story in a new direction? By the mid-point, has the protagonist changed in some significant way?

- Does the conflict for the protagonist and antagonist escalate through the story and as a result of their actions (what one does creates more conflict for the other)?

- Are you giving specific details that reflect upon who your characters really are? (Not just a gun, but what type of gun they carry, for example.)

- Are your symbols or motifs consistent?

CHAPTER 22
TO HAVE AND TO HOLD[19]:
DON'T HOLD ON TO IT, GET IT OUT

STEP 10: SUBMIT, SURVIVE & START AGAIN
"Try Again. Fail Again. Fail Better." --Samuel Beckett

One you've revised and polished your manuscript, let others read it.   First, getting feedback from others is the best way to improve your writing.   Second, even if you're goal isn't to be published by a publishing house, writers generally write to be read. A readership is the ultimate payoff for a writer. Knowing that a reader has connected with your story, heard your message, and been moved by your words will only motivate you to get your next story out.

If you're not interested in getting published in the traditional way, what about printing out your story, posting it on your website or even self-publishing it? This way, even though you have no plans of making your writing a career, you're still getting the satisfaction of a readership.

If your goal is to get published, you'll want to query agents or editors who might be interested in representing you and your work, or even publishing it. Some publishing houses do not require your work to be submitted by an agent for them to consider it for publication. Some do.

---

[19]   *To Have And To Hold* by Patricia Gafney

If you are looking for an agent, the typical thing to do is research which agents represent your type of story and whom you might want to work with. You can talk to other writers or research them on the Web. Then you'll want to "query" the agent. This is normally done with a written query letter, submitted either by snail mail or via email, depending on the agency's preferences.

Although people often agonize about how best to write a query letter, we've generally found that simplicity, professionalism and clarity are what agents and editors are looking for. In general, they'd rather receive plain white paper rather than intricate or perfumed stationary. Some might like it if you compare your work to something that's already popular (because it shows you know where your book fits), while others find this annoying or presumptuous.

What they all want to see, however, is a concise summary of who you are, why you're contacting them (because you're seeking representation or publication), what your story is about (in something that resembles a back cover blurb, which is more than a log line but far less than a synopsis), what your previous writing credentials are, if any, and how to contact you.

Most people typically query multiple agents. You can also explore agents by "pitching" to agents at conferences. A pitch is an opportunity to verbally tell an agent or editor about yourself and your current manuscript. Pitch appointments are typically short, about ten minutes long. If an agent is interested in seeing your work as a result of a pitch appointment, he/she will ask you to submit the manuscript. Usually they ask for a partial of the manuscript first (a synopsis and the first three chapters). If they are still interested after reading the partial, they may ask you to send them the full manuscript. If you get a request, be sure to submit a query letter along with the submission and remind the agent how you met. Also, write "requested material" on the outside of the envelope so it doesn't get thrown into a slush pile (a stack of unsolicited manuscripts that pile up in an agent or editor's office).

This same process applies for editors. You can query editors who take unagented submissions directly. Or you can pitch to an editor at a conference in the hopes that they'll request your manuscript.

Caveat: An important thing to remember with editors, however, is that you may pitch to an editor who does not have the final say in whether to buy a book or not. The editor might be a junior editor that needs to get the approval of a senior editor. Or the editor simply might not have buying authority for a particular line. It is important to research editors so you can realistically determine your chances of selling your manuscript. Of course, finding any editor who loves your work and will champion it is a huge accomplishment!

Once you start submitting, it's important to expect rejections. Don't let them diminish the value you attribute to your work and don't take rejections personally. It's just how the business works. Selling a novel, even one that is indisputably well-written, is hard work. You can do everything you're supposed to and still get a rejection. The great thing about expecting rejections is that you can have a game plan for when you receive them.

Since we're talking about querying an agent or editor, let's talk about what an agent or editor wants. Knowing this might, after all, impact your communication with them. We like what J.A. Konrath, author of *The Newbie's Guide To Publishing*, identifies: 1) a book they can sell; 2) a writer who's easy to work with; 3) a writer who can accept advice and criticism; 4) a writer who understands the market; 5) a writer who can meet a deadline; 6) a writer who is in it for the long haul; 7) a writer who doesn't call and pester them constantly; and 8) a writer who is grateful.

That said, what should you be able to expect from an agent? If you're working with an agent, that agent should, at a minimum, return your calls and emails; let you know when she submits your manuscript and to whom; forward rejections and feedback on your manuscript; and submit manuscripts within a few weeks of accepting them. Ideally, they will be interested in what you want to do next and give you advice. Likewise, an editor will hopefully return your calls and emails; keep you informed of deadlines and release dates; give timely feedback on how to improve your story; and again, take interest in how you want to build your career, develop new stories, and expand your readership

Finally, once you get your work out there, your task is to try not to obsess about your submissions (we know that's hard sometimes!) or how well your current book is selling (assuming you've done what you should to promote it). Your task is to write the next story (we know that's hard, too!). After completing one story, you might wonder how you'll be able to write another one. Believe us, you can. It's in you.

There's always another story to tell (and sell).

FEEDBACK: SO...WHAT DO YOU THINK?

Beyond the basic creative need and drive for self- expression, we write so people will read our story. We want them to love it enough to buy it. Then after they buy it, we want them to love our voice and style enough to keep on buying more. And yet, having people read our work is one of the most nerve-racking aspects of writing.

There's often a natural flow to our readership exposure. We might start with friends and loved ones reading our work. These are usually people who love us and are good at giving warm fuzzies. Usually, the critical feedback is minimal and the encouragement tremendous.

Then we get a little more serious. We want to be authors. Maybe we join RWA and maybe we find a writer group. We start talking to other writers. It's in this phase that we tend to develop critique relationships. Maybe we join a critique group or find a critique partner (or multiple partners... Not a kinky thing in this case!).

At this point, we might enter contests for feedback. We might start submitting our stories to editors and/or agents. We're looking to make our story as strong as possible so we can sell it.

And then, once we sell, we enter a whole new world of feedback - reviews, readers and reactions - Oh my!

So how do we use these phases to our advantage? Each one can give us huge advantages, and each one has the potential to derail and devastate us.

CHEERLEADERS

Moms are great. For the most part, they are supportive and nurturing and quick to point out when the pants we're wearing make our butt look big. But for literary feedback, generally speaking mom falls into the cheerleader category. This goes for friends, other family members, and husbands and wives. This can be a great place to dip your toes into—i.e., the "other people are reading my work" pool. Of course, this can also create a quagmire of problems. The thing about family is that sometimes they aren't supportive. We might not get approving pats –and depending on what we write, we might not feel comfortable having family members read our work. If you think your loved ones will be supportive and excited for you, then by all means, share your story with them. But don't put yourself in the position of courting rejection and hurt feelings if you're concerned that they'll be upset about your chosen genre. For example, an avid mystery and thriller reader, Tawny's grandma never approved of her love of the romance genre, but once she'd sold, grandma did buy a special shelf to hold all of Tawny's (unread) books.

Another caution when it comes to cheerleaders: those closest to us often think they know what's best and want what's best for us. But quite often they don't actually know much about the publishing industry and the realities that you, as a writer, have discovered. So remember who the expert is when they're offering advice and take it with a loving grain of salt.

And lastly, the pursuit of a writing career can be an emotional roller coaster that sucks up huge amounts of time and energy. Any writing loop will share countless stories of family support, and just as many stories of the lack of support writers get from their husbands/wives or kids. We all have to gauge our audience carefully. If you don't have the level of support you'd like, one option would be to sit down and have a serious conversation about what a writing career means to you. In other words, ask for the support you're not getting. Another option would be to accept that this is your journey and you'll be trekking it alone. And, of course, there are many shades of gray between the two options. The important thing is to figure out exactly what level of support you have from the cheerleaders in your life, and to work your writing around that.

TEAM PLAYERS

Once we get serious about writing, we start looking for feedback. Some of the most common ways to get that feedback are through critique groups, critique partners and writing contests. There are benefits and cautions for all three, of course.

CRITIQUE GROUPS

Benefits

- Group energy often keeps people engaged and moving forward
- Different people have different critiquing strengths, which gives a wider range of feedback

Cautions

- Too many cooks ruin the broth – and too many opinions can   confuse an author
- You have to wait your turn for feedback

CRITIQUE PARTNERS

Benefits

- Someone who knows your voice and strengths and helps you build on them
- One on one feedback

Cautions

- Sometimes it takes awhile to find the right partner
- CP relationships can become co-dependent unless both partners are focused on helping each other succeed

CONTESTS

Benefits

- The chance to look for story issues by watching for consistent suggestions (for instance, if three judges mention pacing, it's a definite issue)

- A good way to get your work in front of a variety of readers and possibly editors or agents if you final

Cautions

- The anonymous nature of contests lends itself to a certain amount of snarky feedback

- Revising a manuscript over and over via contest feedback (any feedback, actually) can revise the voice right out of the story

Feedback is essential. Too often, we're so close to our manuscripts that we don't have enough objectivity to see what our story needs. Good feedback can help us strengthen the story, polish our prose and find our voice.

The big caution with all feedback from team players is to be very aware of whether or not the people are really on your team or not. Is their feedback aimed at helping you improve your story? Are they interested in supporting your career decisions, in helping you to make a sale or revise a manuscript to suit a request? Keep in mind, just because they are on your team doesn't mean the feedback will be all warm and fuzzy. But if they are on your team, you should be able to see the benefit to your story, to your writing and to your career if you choose to use their feedback. If you find that there is a consistent lack of benefit, then you might want to ask yourself why you're still playing with them.

COACHES

Editors and agents are the people who impact your career. They are the ones who decide if you get to play on the team or not. As you progress with your writing, you'll find yourself getting revision requests or comments via contests, or perhaps editor critiques. Keep in mind that these people know what they're doing. An editor knows what's selling at their house or line. They see which books work and which tank. And they don't have the spare time to waste asking for revisions if they don't think the story has enough potential for them to buy. So if they offer feedback, it's always worth considering. And if they ask for revisions, it's doubly worth considering.

Once you've sold your book, chances are you'll be asked to do revisions. Give yourself time to understand exactly what your editor is looking for and if you're not sure, get clarification. You both have the same goal--to make the book the strongest it can be and to sell a lot of copies. Working together will help you achieve that.

FANS

After books hit the shelves, it's all about the readers and reviewers. Readers talk to other readers and share their favorite books. Reviewers have a strong voice that reaches even more readers. But here's the thing to remember... after your book is published, it's done. You can't use this feedback to go back and make changes. Disagreeing with a review or arguing with readers or reviewers about story points rarely reflects positively on the author. Our advice is to take this phase of feedback with a grain of salt. Read reviews and ask yourself if there is something that can help you improve your next book. Look for quotes to use in promotion. But don't let reviews derail your writing.

The bottom line is that feedback is a vital part of the writing process. Whatever form you choose to use, make it work for you. But always remember to stay true to your story, to your writing style and to your voice.

PART II:

SEEING HOW IT'S DONE

CHAPTER 23
DECONSTRUCTING A PUBLISHED PLOT

Virna first met Lori Wilde at the Calgary RWA's Crossing The Threshold Conference in 2006. A couple of years later, when Virna was feeling battered by the publishing industry and struggling with completing her third manuscript, she saw that Lori Wilde was offering an online critique class--an opportunity to work with her "one-on-one" for one month. Signing up for that class was one of Virna's wiser decisions.

Lori is a master at her craft. So many times during that month, Virna literally slapped her hand to her forehead and thought, "Are you kidding me? How come someone didn't explain this to me sooner?"

With Lori Wilde's permission, we're analyzing her book, You Only Love Twice ("YOLT"; 2006 by Warner Books) in order to show "real life" application of many of the concepts we've talked about in Part I. YOLT is a lighter romantic suspense.

ABOUT LORI WILDE:

Lori Wilde has written fifty-three novels for three major New York Publishing houses. She holds a bachelors degree in nursing from Texas Christian University and a certificate in forensics. She volunteers as a sexual assault first responder for Freedom House, a shelter for battered women.

Recently, she received a two-book contract from Warner books based solely on a 25-word "high concept" pitch. Her workbook, "Got High Concept?" is a staple in the writing community. She is an instructor for a company that provides online community education to over 1500 colleges and universities.

Lori Wilde writes both category romances for Harlequin Blaze and sexy contemporaries for Avon.

BACK COVER BLURB FOR YOU ONLY LOVE TWICE:

"Comic-book heroine Angelina Avenger battles dastardly criminals and alien invasions. But her creator Marlie Montague's life isn't as exciting...until Marlie opens the front door and finds the business end of a pistol pointed right at her. Her plan: to channel Angelina fast! Recruiting her new next-door neighbor who looks like a rock-hard action hero, couldn't hurt either...

The last thing Navy Secret agent Joel Hunter expected on this surveillance gig was a luscious brunette bursting through his window. Now he and Marlie are blowing the doors off a full-blown conspiracy with more double agents than a Bond flick. But in between shootouts and squealing tires, the mystery that is Marlie is making Joel's heart go *thump thump thump*. Is she a femme fatale or an endearing bookworm? And how does she leave him both shaken and stirred?"

Now doesn't this sound like a fun, sexy book? This is the kind of description that would be appropriate for your query letter to an agent or editor. You want to describe your story in your query letter, but in a way that showcases your voice and the tone of the book.

CHARACTERS
- Marlie Montague – heroine/protagonist
- Joel Hunter – hero/romantic antagonist
- Unidentified Gunman/Abel Johnson– external antagonist/Gus's assistant

- Chet Delaney — external antagonist, Joel's ex-father-in-law
- Augustus Hunter – Joel's father
- Daniel Montague – Marlie's father
- Penelope Montague – Marlie's mother
- Treeni Delaney– Joel's ex-wife
- Cosmo Villereal – Marlie's best friend
- Ronald McDonald (who had the name before the clown) – red herring antagonist

SYNOPSIS

The following synopsis for YOLT was written using the method described in Part I, Step 7 above.

1.   *Establish the goal, motivation, and Internal and External Conflicts of the hero and heroine (and possibly the antagonist). Specify what gets the hero and heroine together romantically, if different. Explain how their Incorrect Core Beliefs rub against each other, but what keeps them together anyway:*

Marlie Montague illustrates controversial, some might even say subversive, comic books with a kick-butt heroine named Angelina Avenger. Because her father was framed as a traitor and killed by his best friend, Augustus Hunter, she doesn't trust easily. Her lack of trust increases when she receives a death threat. Marlie has taken to isolating herself in her house (going so far as to dress and decorate in black and white) when someone knocks on her door. Caution turns into flustered uncertainty when she looks through her peephole and sees her hot neighbor standing on her doorstep. Stalling, Marlie goes to the bathroom to "freshen up." When she returns to answer the door, however, she finds her neighbor has been replaced by a UPS man with a gun.

Joel Hunter, Marlie's neighbor, knows Marlie has reason to be wary of him, even if she doesn't quite know why. Joel's father,

Gus, and Marlie's father, Daniel, used to be friends until Daniel was accused of selling Mohawk missiles to terrorists and Gus, a military officer, accidentally shot him during his apprehension. Afterwards, Joel's parents divorced, and he followed in his father's footsteps and pursued a Navy career. Recently, he was kicked out of the Navy SEALs after his ex-wife Treeni was hurt trying to disarm some missiles without proper authorization; to protect her, Joel took the blame. His ex-father-in-law, Chet Delaney, pulled some strings and Joel now works for the Naval Criminal Investigative Service. He's been assigned the task of watching Marlie for subversive activities.

Joel doesn't want anything to do with his current assignment: first, he thinks it's a waste of time, and second, he suspects Delaney assigned him to Marlie to keep him away from his ex-wife, Treeni. Unfortunately, his superiors won't relieve him. Instead, they've ordered him not only to spy on Marlie, but to actually befriend her. Part of him is relieved when he rings her doorbell and she fails to answer. Joel returns home.

Then, just when Joel gets out of the shower and is wearing nothing but a towel, Marlie bursts into his house, claiming she's just fought off a man with a gun. She's hurt. Joel, not sure what to believe about her armed gunman, nonetheless treats her wounds. In the process, he finds his attraction for Marlie is greater than even he bargained for. After Marlie tells Joel what happened, he calls the police. The cop who shows up, however, is biased against Marlie and doesn't believe her story about the gunman.

2. *Next, show the development of the hero and heroine's romantic relationship even as the stakes of the external plot rise. Show the progression to the Midpoint, including their first kiss and how they slowly begin to reveal their secrets. Show what happens in the external plot to make the protagonist commit 100% at the Midpoint:*

Not liking the way the officer is treating Marlie, Joel comes to her rescue by standing up to the officer. Unfortunately, Marlie isn't willing to trust him and sends him on his way. Now that he's talked to her again, Joel isn't willing to let her go so easily.

Determined to stay close to her, and knowing she plans on visiting her mother, he immobilizes her car by tampering with the tires, then offers her a ride. Marlie accepts, but only because she's worried about her mother. Before accepting a ride, however, Marlie gathers evidence from her slashed tires and sends it to a friend to process.

During the ride to Marlie's mom's house, Marlie and Joel reveal more about themselves. Specifically, Marlie confesses her belief that love isn't worth the hurt it ultimately causes. She also reveals a crush she had on a boy when she was younger, unwittingly revealing the crush had been on Joel. This knowledge simply makes Joel more determined to explore his attraction to Marlie.

Unfortunately, when they arrive at Marlie's mom's house, they discover her missing and her house ransacked. Marlie is so emotionally overwrought, Joel gives her some whisky. She drinks more than she should and promptly throws up. While she's recovering, smoke fills the house. Someone has set it on fire. Marlie inhales too much smoke, and Joel is forced to drag her to safety and give her CPR. When the police arrive and Marlie is revived, she sees her would-be assassin from earlier that morning. Joel gives chase, but the gunman jumps into his black Camaro and takes off.

Not to be left wringing her hands, Marlie hotwires Joel's car to go after the Camaro. During the chase, she reveals a daring side, one that Joel clearly admires. Just as she's about to follow the gunman by jumping a bridge, she suddenly comes to her senses and stops the car. She and Joel are so pumped up with adrenalin that they kiss. The sexual contact is explosive, causing Marlie to pull back in fear. At that time, she realizes that Joel has been shot. She drives him to a hospital. Before he can be treated, they discover Marlie is now wanted by the police. Joel's boss orders him to bring Marlie in. Believing that his boss is biased against her and that Marlie is truly in danger, Joel refuses.

3. *Next, show the escalating stakes in the External Conflict and how it causes the romantic conflict to breakdown. Show the hero and heroine revealing their true natures more and more, and how this increases their physical intimacy, as well:*

In order to avoid the police as well as Joel's superiors, Joel takes Marlie to his father's place on Mustang Island. Once there, Marlie sews up Joel's wounds. Forced to be together in close quarters, Joel and Marlie reveal the circumstances of their past wounds, including the reason for his divorce and the reason why she doesn't trust anyone. They become even more physically intimate, but Marlie pulls away in fear. That's when Marlie sees a face in the window. Joel chases the man down, only to discover he has some connection to the Navy. Even more disturbing is the man's babbling about a boy and murder. Fearing that his father's house has been compromised, Joel drives Marlie to an isolated floating warehouse owned by her friend, Cosmo.

Not sure who to trust now, but believing Marlie's comics might give them a clue, Joel goes back to her house to get them. When they meet up, Joel gives Marlie a gift--a pretty, frilly dress that shows her how sexy he thinks she is. Believing that Joel is the one man she can trust, Marlie gives herself to him and they have sex. Although he relishes their new closeness, Joe worries that he hasn't told her who he really is or that he's a spy.

4.   *Finally, show the protagonist's greatest fear come true, and how this causes her to pull away from the hero and retreat back into "Identity" (her mask/Incorrect Core Beliefs). Describe how she comes to some realization that prompts her to face her greatest fear and show that her change/Character Arc is now permanent. Explain that, because of her willingness to change, she is able to face and defeat the antagonist, transform her life for the better, and get her happy ending:*

Before he can tell Marlie who he is, Marlie gets the results from her tampered tires. She discovers that Joel slashed her tires, but even worse, he's a spy and the same boy she used to have a crush on so long ago. Feeling humiliated and betrayed, Marlie handcuffs Joel to the bed and leaves.

Furious but unable to escape, Joel picks up one of Marlie's comic books, skims it, and realizes she might have been targeted because of something she illustrated. Soon, Marlie's friend, Cosmo, and Joel's ex-wife, Treeni, who have been piecing together clues on their own, find Joel and reveal several shocking truths: that Delaney, Treeni's father, has been storing defective Mohawk missiles and selling them, and that Gus, Joel's father, found the remote launching code and is now missing.

Frantic, Joel calls his father's assistant, Abel Johnson, who tells him that Gus is in trouble. Following Gus's orders, Abel removed several confidential documents from Gus's safe. Abel agrees to meet Joel to give him the documents. When they meet, Joel discovers that Abel is the owner of the black Camaro and is looking for Gus in order to avenge his own father's death. He tells Joel that Marlie's father faked his death after he, Gus, and Delaney covered up the death of Abel's father by one of Delaney's defective missiles. Abel forces Joel to drive to a bunker where Daniel, and Penelope, Marlie's missing mother, are hiding. Gus is also there, trying to warn Daniel.

Although Marlie had devised a comic book plot where her heroine, Angelina, discovered her father had faked his own death, Marlie has no idea her own father is alive. She returns to her mother's house to search for clues. On the way, she sees Joel and

Abel, the man with the black Camaro. Not sure what to think, she follows them to the bunker. From what she knows about him, she can't believe Joel is working in league with the assassin and is determined to save him. Marlie pulls a smoke-bomb, which she carries around with her for emergencies, from her purse. She throws it into the bunker and tackles Abel. Joel helps subdue him.

Marlie finds out her father is alive. She is shocked and overjoyed. Abel uses this to his advantage, getting free long enough to shoot Marlie in the back.

Marlie recovers from her wounds. At the end of the story, Marlie no longer sees things in black and white and she doesn't dress that way any more either. Her world has color again. Her father is alive and his reputation is cleared along with Joel's. Moreover, Joel reveals he's kept a baseball card from his youth; the card is proof-positive that he'd had a crush on her, too. The missiles are kept out of the terrorist's hands, Delaney is court-martialed, and Joel and Marlie get their happy ending.

SINGLE TITLE ROMANTIC SUSPENSE

You Only Love Twice is a single title romantic suspense. It's published by Warner Books, is not part of a serial imprint, and is 325 pages. It has a romance at its core, supplemented by several suspenseful elements—Will Marlie and Joel outrun the killer? Will they find out why he's trying to kill Marlie? Will they find Marlie's mother?

GETTING TO THE STORY QUESTION IN YOLT:

Before page eight of Wilde's book, the reader learns about Marlie's Ordinary World. She's a comic book illustrator who's been working all day, is wearing glasses and a tracksuit, and is shy and withdrawn despite having a kick-butt alter ego who prods her to be more daring. Her father was a government whistle-blower who'd been killed under suspicious circumstances and she believes he was falsely accused of selling terrorists Mohawk missiles.

On page eight, the Inciting Incident occurs, thrusting Marlie out of her Ordinary World and into the new world of the story-- she answers her front door to find a man pointing a gun at her. Within the next few chapters, we know the Story Question:

Will Marlie Montague defeat the man trying to kill her and get her goal of staying alive and saving her mother, who has been kidnapped?

THE THEME IN YOLT

1. Intent/Global Message: Wilde's intent in writing the novel is to convey a mood of humor, sensuality, and action. Even from the back cover blurb, it is obvious she succeeds. This is also obvious by her opening line:

"Marlie Montague was right smack-dab in the middle of exposing a massive government cover-up when her front doorbell chimed, playing the Mission: Impossible theme."

Okay, so we don't quite get a sense of sensuality yet, but it's obvious from the first line that this story is going to be action-packed and humorous, right? The sensuality comes soon after! Here's one of my favorite passages, in which Lori Wilde uses a character's "silence" to convey deep emotion:

"[Marlie] wasn't the only one totally blown away. Eddies of embarrassment and sexual hunger washed over her, warring waves of boldness and timidity.

'Joel...' What was she going to say? That she was sorry? But she had nothing to apologize for. He had kissed her.

She reached out, not knowing what she intended to do, but got caught up in the crazy push-pull battle inside her.

But Joel raised an arm, blocking her hand, and latched his eyes on hers.

He was breathing hard and he did not speak. He didn't have to speak. She could read the message in his eyes loud and clear.

Come any closer, touch me again, and I will have no choice but to take you right here, right now, the rest of the world be damned."

2. Thematic message (conclusion about life and humanity) that Lori Wilde proves throughout her story: "In order to find true love, you must take a leap of faith."

Just by reading the above synopsis, we know Lori Wilde proves her Theme by rewarding Marlie for her increasing willingness to take a leap of faith. Not only does she get Joel, she gets her father and mother back, she defeats the bad guys, and she makes the world a safer place.

More specifically, Wilde spells out the Theme for the reader on page five. At this point, after seeing Joel at the door, Marlie is tempted to "slink back" and pretend she never heard the doorbell ring. Marlie engages in a mental argument with her alter ego, Angelina Avenger:

"You're being paranoid again, Angelina chided. This guy has nothing to do with those death threats or what the Navy did to your dad. Open the door.

'Easy for you to say; you're a fearless crime fighter.'

Don't give me that b.s. You're not afraid that Mr. Hunka Man came over here to do you harm. You're just too chicken to talk to him.

There was that.

Marlie's natural impulse urged her to slink back to her office and pretend she'd never heard the Mission: Impossible theme summoning her to the front door. She had a deadline looming and three pages left to illustrate before tackling the computer phase.

That's right. Go ahead. Blame it on your work. Never mind that you're hiding behind your shyness as an excuse to avoid getting a real life. And maybe, just maybe, a real man."

Despite herself, Marlie feels "an odd sensation, pushing up from somewhere deep inside her, daring her to open the door."

Notice how Wilde is able to state her Theme by creating Angelina, Marlie's alter ego, who lays out Marlie's Internal Conflict (fear of trusting anyone) for the reader. Angelina is telling Marlie the very thing that Lori Wilde is asserting to the reader — that trusting and taking a leap of faith will make her life so much better than it is.

We'll discuss the ways Wilde *proves* her Theme below.

CREATE A TAGLINE, LOG LINE, STORY PREMISE AND HIGH CONCEPT PITCH IF POSSIBLE

- Possible tagline:

He's a spy assigned to watch her, but is she a femme fatale or an endearing bookworm?

- Possible Log line:

A frumpy, introverted comic book illustrator must channel her inner superwoman in order to outrun a man determined to kill her, rescue her missing mother, and keep up with her sexy neighbor, whose military background stands for everything she mistrusts.

- Marlie's Premise:

In order to learn to trust and take a leap of faith, Marlie Montague must learn to set free her "inner superwoman," trust a spy whose been assigned to watch her, and put everything on the line to stop the bad guys.

EXPANDING UPON YOLT'S THEME AND USING MOTIF AND SYMBOLS

- Theme

As noted earlier, Wilde's thematic message in YOLT is that in order to find love, a person must take a leap of faith. Wilde reveals her Theme in several ways, including at page 65 when Marlie tells Joel: "I don't take anything on faith." Joel, however, sees how Marlie is internally torn.

"He saw the longing in her eyes and knew she wanted to trust him but simply couldn't bring herself to do it. She wasn't one to let down her guard easily."

As the reader, we know that Wilde is going to challenge Marlie's mistrust over and over again in order to get her to change. Why? Because that's what Marlie needs to be happy.

Wilde proves her Theme throughout her story.

First, she creates a foil for her thematic assertion by giving the reader a glimpse into Marlie's Ordinary World. Marlie dresses in black and white, and decorates her house in black and white. Marlie favors black and white because it has no ambiguity. "It's either one or the other." In other words, she knows exactly what she's getting and doesn't have to take a risk. Joel, on the other hand, sees how she "isolated herself even in her own home. He could almost touch her loneliness." Through Joel's eyes, we know that Marlie's lack of trust is holding her back from having a happy life.

Then, Wilde puts events in motion so Marlie is forced to overcome her fear of trusting. As the reader cheers her on, Wilde also proves her Theme in subtext. She does this by showing the positive effects of trusting/taking a leap of faith, as well as by showing the negative consequences of not doing this.

For example, in her first scene, Marlie's inability to trust causes her to delay answering the door when Joel comes to visit her. As a result, when she finally does answer the door, Joel is gone and in his place is a man pointing a gun at her.

Later, when Marlie overcomes her instinct to cower or be passive and instead fights the gunman, she is able to escape; her reward (although she doesn't necessarily think of it this way at first) is getting into Joel's house and finding him in just a towel.

Even Wilde's secondary characters prove the Theme. When Marlie's mother foregoes thoughts of suicide and takes another chance at life, she is rewarded by a phone call from her "dead" husband. He ends up "kidnapping" her (she loves him but she's a little shocked to see him since he's supposed to be dead).

In addition, Cosmo, Marlie's best friend, decides to make a move on Treeni even though she's out of his league and has a bad reputation. His ability to take a leap of faith is rewarded when she tells him to come back to her house with her. They uncover her father's treachery and ultimately are key to helping Joel and Marlie defeat Abel Johnson and Delaney.

- Motif

Wilde establishes a motif throughout YOLT that is significant given Marlie's career (illustrator of a comic with a superwoman protagonist) and her premise (that she needs to take a leap of faith by freeing and revealing her own superwoman). The motif is "heroes," which she showcases several ways.

First, with the very first line of her book, she has Marlie's doorbell play the Mission: Impossible Theme song. She emphasizes the tune five separate times within the first eight pages.

Then, throughout the book, she makes several references to different type of heroes and/or crime solvers, including Magnum P.I., Nancy Drew, and John F. Kennedy. At different points in the story, she has Marlie hum the song "Holding Out For A Hero," think of Joel as a hero, or remind herself that she needs to be her own hero. In addition, she imbues Joel with what he considers to be a flaw: an internal drive to protect a woman in need.

"Whenever a vulnerable woman's face beseeched, "Can I get a hero," Joel could never refuse the call."

Good thing for Marlie, right?

- Symbols

The smoke bomb Marlie carries around in her purse "just in case" is a foreshadowing symbol of her willingness to take a leap of faith—she keeps it in reserve, but when she needs it, she pulls it out.

The dress that Joel buys her is symbolic of his desire for her, and how he sees her as having so many more possibilities than she herself believes.

The fact Marlie dresses in black and white, and decorates her apartment in black and white, is symbolic of her closed-off, untrusting nature at the beginning of the book. The way her world transforms to include color after she meets Joel is symbolic of her willingness to open herself to others, and the joy (and risk) life has to offer.

CONFLICT IN YOLT

Wilde establishes Internal, External and Romantic Conflict that gets in the way of Marlie's goals and causes her to adapt, reflect and change.

- Marlie's initial conscious goal: Turn in her next comic book on time; Motivation: It's how she makes a living; Conflict: Someone comes to her door wanting to kill her.

- Marlie's subconscious goal (the internal goal that Wilde has in store for her): To live a more exciting life, to clear her father's name, and to fall in love; Motivation: These are things she needs to be complete; Conflict: She does not trust and is unwilling to take risks.

- Marlie's External Conflict: Someone tries to kill Marlie; someone has kidnapped her mother; the police think Marlie and Joel are criminals.

- Marlie's Internal Conflict: Marlie has a hard time trusting others as well as herself. She's torn between her need to be cautious and her alter ego's need to be daring. This is something Wilde reveals through others' eyes, including Angelina the Avenger and Joel. As Joel recognizes, "It was almost as if [Marlie] were alternating between two characters, the timid, caring hermit and the bold, calculating adventuress."

- Marlie and Joel's Romantic Conflict: Joel is hiding the fact that he and Marlie were friends as children, and that he is a spy assigned to watch her. Marlie does not trust anyone associated with the military and does not trust love in general because she's afraid of being hurt the way her mother was when her father died.

- Marlie's end conscious goal: To stay alive, to save her mother, to trust her instincts. Ultimately, she wants to save Joel and have her HEA; Motivation: She wants to stay alive and loves her mother, she loves Joel, and she wants to be happy; Conflict: the bad guys are still after them; she doubts herself and has a hard time taking risks.

PLOT (CONFLICT BETWEEN PROTAGONIST AND ANTAGONIST FORCES ACTION)

Wilde insures that the conflict Marlie encounters is conflict caused by herself and her own doubt (inner antagonist), Joel (the romantic antagonist), and Delaney/Abel Johnson (the external plot antagonists). Each of these antagonists push and pull at Marlie, who then responds. This is apparent when we analyze Lori Wilde's book for Three Act Structure below.

BREAKING DOWN PLOT WITH THE THREE ACT STRUCTURE

Wilde's story follows the Three Act Structure beautifully. Let's look at synopsis we wrote above and show you how that synopsis includes all the major stages and Turning Points in it. This isn't a coincidence, by the way. A synopsis is a perfect tool for showing an agent or editor that you can structure a novel to include all the major Turning Points.

- STAGE 1: SET UP/VIEW INTO THE PROTAGONIST'S ORDINARY WORLD

Marlie Montague illustrates controversial, some might even say subversive, comic books with a kick-butt heroine named Angelina Avenger. Because her father was framed as a traitor and killed by his best friend, Augustus Hunter, she doesn't trust easily. Her lack of trust increases when she receives a death threat. Marlie has taken to isolating herself in her house when someone knocks on her door. Caution turns into flustered uncertainty when she looks through her peephole and sees her hot neighbor standing on her doorstep.

- Turing Point 1: (OPPORTUNITY FORCES CHARACTER INTO ACTION AND STARTS CONFLICT)

Stalling, Marlie goes to the bathroom to "freshen up." When she returns to answer the door, however, she finds her neighbor has been replaced by a UPS man with a gun.

- STAGE 2: PROGRESS

Joel Hunter, Marlie's neighbor, knows Marlie has reason to be wary of him, even if she doesn't quite know why. Joel's father, Gus, and Marlie's father, Daniel, used to be friends until Daniel was accused of selling Mohawk missiles to terrorists and Gus accidentally shot him during his apprehension. Afterwards, Joel's parents divorced, and he followed in his father's footsteps and pursued a Navy Career. Recently, he was kicked out of the Navy Seals after his ex-wife Treeni was hurt trying to disarm some missiles without proper authorization; to protect her, Joel took the blame. His ex-father-in-law, Chet Delaney, pulled some strings and Joel now works for the Naval Criminal Investigative Service. He's been assigned the task of watching Marlie for subversive activities.

Joel doesn't want anything to do with his current assignment: first, he thinks it's a waste of time, and second, he suspects Delaney assigned him to Marlie to keep him away from his ex-wife, Treeni. Unfortunately, his superiors won't relieve him. Instead, they've ordered him not only to spy on Marlie, but to actually befriend her. Part of him is relieved when he rings her doorbell and she fails to answer. Joel returns home.

Then, just when Joel gets out of the shower and is wearing nothing but a towel, Marlie bursts into his house, claiming she's just fought off a man with a gun. She's hurt. Joel, not sure what to believe about her armed gunman, nonetheless treats her wounds.

In the process, he finds his attraction for Marlie is greater than even he bargained for. After Marlie tells Joel what happened, he calls the police. The cop who shows up, however, is biased against Marlie and doesn't believe her story about the gunman.

Not liking the way the officer is treating Marlie, Joel comes to her rescue. Unfortunately, Marlie isn't willing to trust him and sends him on his way.

- Turning Point 2: (SOMETHING UNEXPECTED HAPPENS, LIKELY THE FIRST DEFEAT, RESULTS IN CHANGE OF PLANS OR GOAL)

Determined to stay close to her, and knowing she plans on visiting her mother, he immobilizes her car, then offers her a ride. Marlie accepts, but only because she's worried about her mother. Before accepting a ride, however, Marlie gathers evidence from her slashed tires and sends it to a friend to process.

During the ride to Marlie's mom's house, Marlie and Joel reveal more about themselves. Specifically, Marlie confesses her belief that love isn't worth the hurt it ultimately causes. She also reveals a crush she had on a boy when she was younger, unwittingly revealing the crush had been on Joel. This knowledge simply makes Joel more determined to explore his attraction to Marlie.

- STAGE 3: INCREASED COMPLICATIONS

Unfortunately, when they arrive at Marlie's mom's house, they discover her missing and her house ransacked. Marlie is so emotionally overwrought, Joel gives her some whisky. She drinks more than she should and promptly throws up. While she's recovering, smoke fills the house. Someone has set it on fire. Marlie inhales too much smoke, and Joel is forced to drag her to safety and give her CPR. When the police arrive and Marlie is revived, she sees her would-be assassin from earlier that morning. Joel gives chase, but the gunman jumps into his black Camaro and takes off.

Not to be left wringing her hands, Marlie hotwires Joel's car to go after the Camaro. During the chase, she reveals a daring side, one that Joel clearly admires. Just as she's about to follow the gunman by jumping a bridge, she suddenly comes to her senses and stops the car. She and Joel are so pumped up with adrenalin that they kiss. The sexual contact is explosive, causing Marlie to pull back in fear.

- Turing Point 3: (GREATER SETBACK RESULTS IN CHARACTER'S FULL COMMITMENT AND TO POINT OF NO RETURN)

At that time, she realizes that Joel has been shot. She drives him to a hospital. Before he can be treated, they discover Marlie is now wanted by the police. Joel's boss orders him to bring Marlie in. Believing that his boss is biased against her and that Marlie is truly in danger, Joel refuses.

In order to avoid the police as well as Joel's superiors, Joel takes Marlie to his father's place on Mustang Island. Once there, Marlie sews up Joel's wounds.

- STAGE 4: FINAL PUSH; PROTAGONIST APPEARS TO BE LOSING

Forced to be together in close quarters, Joel and Marlie reveal the circumstances of their past wounds, including the reason for his divorce and the reason why she doesn't trust anyone. They become even more physically intimate, but Marlie pulls away in fear. That's when Marlie sees a face in the window. Joel chases the man down, only to discover he has some connection to the Navy. Even more disturbing is the man's babbling about a boy and murder. Fearing that his father's house has been compromised, Joel drives Marlie to an isolated floating warehouse owned by her friend.

Not sure who to trust now, but believing Marlie's comics might give them a clue, Joel goes back to her house to get them. When they meet up, Joel gives Marlie a gift--a pretty, frilly dress that shows her how sexy he thinks she is. Believing that Joel is the one man she can trust, Marlie gives herself to him and they have sex. Although he relishes their new closeness, Joe worries that he hasn't told her who he really is or that he's a spy.

- Turning Point 4: (MAJOR SET BACK THAT RESULTS IN THE BLACK MOMENT)

Before he can tell Marlie who he is, Marlie gets the results from her tampered tires. She discovers that Joel is not only a spy, but the same boy she used to have a crush on so long ago. Feeling humiliated and betrayed, Marlie handcuffs Joel to the bed and leaves.

- STAGE 5: REALIZATION/AFTERMATH

Furious but unable to escape, Joel picks up one of Marlie's comic books, skims it, and realizes she might have been targeted because of something she illustrated. Soon, Marlie's friend, Cosmo, and Joel's ex-wife, who have been piecing together clues on their own, find Joel and reveal several shocking truths: that Delaney, Treeni's father, has been storing defective Mohawk missiles and selling them, and that Gus, Joel's father, found the remote launching code and is now missing.

Frantic, Joel calls his father's assistant, Abel Johnson, who tells him that Gus is in trouble. Following Gus's orders, Abel removed several confidential documents from Gus's safe. Abel agrees to meet Joel to give him the documents. When they meet, Joel discovers that Abel is the owner of the black Camaro and is looking for Gus in order to avenge his own father's death. He tells Joel that Marlie's father faked his death after he, Gus, and Delaney covered up the death of Abel's father by one of Delaney's defective missiles. Abel forces Joel to drive to a bunker where Gus, Daniel, and Penelope, Marlie's missing mother, are hiding.

Although Marlie had devised a comic book plot where her heroine, Angelina, discovered her father had faked his own death, Marlie has no idea her own father is alive. She returns to her mother's house to search for clues. On the way, she sees Joel and Abel, the man with the black Camaro. Not sure what to think, she follows them to the bunker. She can't believe Joel is working in league with the assassin and is determined to save him.

- Turning Point 5: (CLIMAX)

Marlie pulls a smoke-bomb, which she carries around with her for emergencies, from her purse. She throws it into the bunker and tackles Abel. Joel helps subdue him.

Marlie finds out her father is alive. She is shocked and overjoyed. Abel uses this to his advantage, getting free long enough to shoot Marlie in the back.

- STAGE 6: RESOLUTION

Marlie recovers from her wounds. At the end of the story, Marlie no longer sees things in black and white, and she doesn't dress that way any more either. Her world has color again. Her father is alive and his reputation is cleared along with Joel's. Moreover, Joel reveals he's kept a baseball card from his youth; the card is proof-positive that he'd had a crush on her, too. The missiles are kept out of the terrorist's hands, Delaney is court-martialed, and Joel and Marlie get their happy ending.

HOW YOLT RAISES THE STAKES IN EVERY SCENE WITH SCENE AND SEQUEL

Analyzing YOLT shows Wilde's scenes: 1) have purpose (further the plot), are told in the POV of the character with the most to lose, and orient the reader as to the scene setting right away; and 2) answer the questions:

1. What is the POV character's scene goal?
2. What is his motivation?
3. What is the Internal and External Conflict getting in the way of the scene goal?
4. Did the POV character get his goal? Answer this with a "Yes, but…" OR "No, and furthermore…" and then add the disaster element at the end of the scene.

Briefly, let's look at how this works.

In Chapter 1, Scene 1, Marlie's goal is to illustrate her comic book. She's motivated by her career and because she lives a life of adventure vicariously through her character, Angelina Avenger. Her conflict is that her neighbor comes to the door and flusters her. At the end of the scene, does Marlie get her goal of illustrating her comic book? The answer is _no, and furthermore_, the scene ends with a disaster—she answers the door and finds not Joel, but another man pointing a gun at her.

Now, let's shift directly to Marlie's next POV scene. Remember, the goal in this next scene is going to be based on the disaster that occurred in the previous scene. So, in Chapter 2, Scene 1, Marlie's goal is to escape the guy with the gun. Her motivation is to survive. Her conflict is that the assassin doesn't want to let her live. She breaks into Joel's house and that's where the scene ends with a disaster. Did she get her goal of escaping the assassin? _Yes, but_ now she's alone in a house with her sexy neighbor who is wearing nothing but a towel. Now, this disaster is not huge and in comparison to having someone point a gun at you, it's not as dire, but the point is Marlie's actions in escaping the gunman have just made her situation a little "worse" (for her peace of mind and in terms of protecting her heart). She is now face-to-face with another type of dangerous male.

Let's do Marlie's next POV scene. In Chapter 3, Scene 2, Marlie's goal is to maintain her cool in front of the naked, hot guy. Her motivation is to keep her pride and protect her heart. Her conflict is that Joel is almost naked, he's tending her wounds, which puts him in close proximity, and she feels vulnerable and shaken after almost being killed. She ends up crying in front of him. So, does Marlie get her goal of maintaining her cool? _No, and furthermore_ the scene ends on a disaster because Joel voices his suspicions about her, making her realize she can't rely on him to help her. Instead, she needs to be wary of him and continue to look out for herself.

From there, the scenes build on each other. The disasters in Marlie's POV spark the goals in her other POV scenes.

RAISED STAKES & DIMINISHED OPTIONS LEAD TO TRANSFORMATION/CHARACTER ARC

As we've seen above by analyzing Wilde's use of the Three Act Structure, the complications in the external plot progress, stakes rise, and Marlie's options diminish the farther the story goes on. We see Marlie's Character Arc from the beginning of the story to the end. She alternately berates herself for being cowardly or for her lack of trust, but she also can't help shying away from conflict or the idea of getting her heart broken. As Joel recognizes at one point, she "talked a good game, but she rattled easy." Nonetheless, it's Marlie's willingness to face her flaws and overcome them that makes us care about her and cheer her on.

ANSWERING THE STORY QUESTION OF WHETHER THE PROTAGONIST ACHIEVED HIS GOAL/HAPPY ENDING

Of course, Wilde gives Marlie her well-deserved happy ending, but she shows the reader how Marlie's world has transformed as a result of the growth she achieved during the story. In addition to showing us how she has changed through her actions, Wilde shows us that Marlie has changed internally — in the second half of the book, Marlie no longer needs to rely on her alter ego, Angelina Avenger, to be daring for her. Rather, she dares on her own.

Lori Wilde's novel, You Only Love Twice, provides a bird's eye view into how a writer can take advantage of so many tools in her arsenal: Conflict, Structure, Theme, Motif, Symbolism, etc. As Wilde herself pointed out, however, these things are tools, not "rules" meant to diminish your options. As Virna was analyzing Wilde's book, she found a couple of scenes that didn't end with a disaster or where Lori strayed from the traditional practice of staying in one person's POV per scene. That's okay. Sometimes your story is going to go places you don't expect because writing is craft and <u>art</u>. You shouldn't try to control things too tightly. Sometimes the muse and your characters will want to do their own thing. However, having a strong game plan and foundation is going to do nothing but help you in the end.

PART III:

THE CHALLENGES AHEAD

CHAPTER 24

SHADES OF TWILIGHT[20]:

AS FAR AS GETTING PUBLISHED, THINK GOOD, BAD, AND SUBJECT TO INTERPRETATION

Common sense indicates, and we've emphasized, that one of the things you need to do to be a successful writer is to *keep writing*. Scene by scene. Chapter by chapter. Manuscript by manuscript. Writing is what makes you a writer.

Perseverance is what makes you talented and successful.

Combining each of these with some luck is what's going to get you published.

What will also help is gathering knowledge about the business side of things and what challenges you may face. If you expect difficult times, you stand a greater chance of not taking them personally. You'll also be less tempted to question your methods, your talent, or your destiny.

---

[20] *Shades Of Twilight* by Linda Howard

REALITY CHICK[21]:

THE TRUTH ABOUT WHO WANTS TO WRITE, WHO REALLY WRITES, WHO GETS PUBLISHED, AND WHO READS PUBLISHED BOOKS

WRITERS:
- 80% of Americans want to write a book
- The average debut author is likely to earn an advance of between $2,000-$20,000 on his or her first book
- The six-figure advance for newer or unknown authors is becoming a myth

READERS:
- Most Americans do not buy or read books
- The average number of books read per year by those people who read regularly is 16 books
- 57% of new books are not read to completion
- Of American readers, 53% read fiction, 43% read nonfiction
- 55% of fiction is bought by women, 45% by men
- Women are said to control 80% of every dollar spent on consumer goods

PUBLISHERS
- 2,000,000 + manuscripts are submitted annually
- Close to 95% of submitted manuscripts are rejected
- Of those, approximately 120,000 new books are published each year in the US

---

21   *Reality Chick* by Lauren Barholdt

- A fiction book is considered successful if it sells 5,000 copies
- 70% of books published do not earn back their advances
- 70% of books do not make a profit

CHAPTER 25
ROCKY ROAD[22]: ONE WRITER'S JOURNEY

If you saw a writer working on a novel, what would you think? When you think of yourself as a writer, how does it make you feel? Do you think writing is fun? Difficult? Joyful? Anxiety producing? Of course, the answer is it's all of these things.

The business side of writing is no different. Agents and editors are going to look at a written work and evaluate whether they can sell it and how much money it's going to make them or their publishing house.

That's their jobs.

They can't be swayed because you poured your heart and soul into your work, or desperately want to grow as a writer and have your book in a bookstore. Moreover, even if they're interested in you and your book, they're going to get back to you on *their* schedule, which is probably going to be a long time.

Longer than you expect.

Maybe, every once in awhile, they'll never get back to you.

Not because they're mean or hated your work. They might not even have read it. Editors and agents are swamped with work and often have to read outside normal business hours. A lot of things fall through the cracks as a result.

So should you write? Once again, the answer is obvious:

If you want to write, write. Don't let the above stop you. Despite everything, you can write and you can sell!

---

22   *Rocky Road* by Anne Stuart

In the next several pages, Virna relates what she learned in the three years it took her to sell her first book. For those of you who want more detail, she'll break things down even more in the appendix of this book. Hopefully, this will give you an idea of what the journey to publication is like (at the very least, what her journey was like).

Writing and getting published happens differently for different people. It will happen differently for you. Just because one person did something one way doesn't mean you should. However, we can always learn from other people's experiences and mistakes, don't you think?

VIRNA'S JOURNEY
FROM BEGINNING HER FIRST STORY TO
GETTING HER FIRST SALE

3 years, 2 months, 12 days
1169 days

Four Years Of National RWA Dues:	$340
Four Years Of Membership In Five Local RWA Chapters:	$500
Over 50 Local RWA Chapter Meetings:	$1000
Three National RWA Conferences Attended:	$3000
10 Local RWA Chapter Retreats or Conferences Attended:	$4000
Two Local Chapter Contests Entered (Placed Second In One):	$50
Three Golden Heart Entries (Never Finaled):	$150
CDs From Two Prior National Conferences Ordered:	$150
One Group Blog Launched:	$500
One Website Designed	$500

And Launched:	
Various Domain Names Purchased:	$200
Five Full Manuscripts Requested – Several Snail Mailed	$50
Ten Online Classes/Workshops Registered For:	$500
Various Agent, Editor, Author Critiques & Networking Opps Purchased via Auctions	$2000
Approximate Total:	$13000
GETTING THE CALL FROM MY AGENT THAT I SOLD:	PRICELESS

BUT Getting to that sale didn't come without an emotional price and personal sacrifice.

BLOOD, SWEAT & TEARS:
- 4 full single title manuscripts written
- 2 full category manuscripts written
- 5 proposals written
- 1 NanoWriMo almost completed
- 2 board positions for local RWA chapter served
- 6 in person pitches to editors
- 4 in person pitches to agents
- 8 email queries to agents
- 2 editors who loved one of my manuscripts and would have bought but ultimately couldn't
- 2 offers of representation by agents
- 1 agent switch
- 40 submissions to editors via agent
- 34 rejections by editors via agent
- Many friends made
- Some friends lost
- Challenges to personal relationships encountered
- 35 pounds gained

WHAT VIRNA LEARNED IN YEAR ONE
- You don't have to be single, be independently wealthy, or quit your day job to write, nor do you need to have majored in creative writing.

- To write, all you need is to sit down and write your story. Of course, you need the drive to work hard, the support to logistically do it, and the willingness to ask for help and learn from the experience of others.

- To be a writer, you should be driven, but you can also be flexible; setting a schedule or writing an outline gives you a roadmap, but it doesn't have to lock you in.

- Pursuing writing, as with any creative endeavor, will benefit you in other aspects of your life. For example, I had to get over my fear of flying in order to attend conferences.

- The women in RWA are passionate, talented, supportive, and plain old fun to be around.
- You can take risks and break the rules, and sometimes it will pay off.
- Just because you have interest in a book or what seems like an offer, an agent won't necessarily take you on.
- Sometimes, in combination with hard work, the stars will align early on.

WHAT VIRNA LEARNED IN YEAR TWO

- Heartache is a natural part of the business and sometimes waiting to get a rejection is preferable to several in a row.
- You can survive rejection by moving forward and continuing to work on the next project, and keeping busy will pay off.
- Despite how good you think you are, you can always improve.
- Despite setbacks, if you persist and prepare, you will see positive results.
- Even if an editor wants to buy your work, she might not be the editor who makes the decision.
- Circumstances and individual needs change. Pay attention to why you're uncomfortable with professional or personal relationships. Try to make small changes before doing something drastic.

WHAT VIRNA LEARNED IN YEAR THREE

- Sometimes, combining strengths with others will get you through difficult times.

- It's never too early to prepare to be published, which includes developing a website/web presence.

- A situation that another person envies still might not be the right situation for you. You can take advice from others but ultimately you have to trust your instincts, even if everyone else thinks you're crazy (and sometimes you do, too).

- Always try to act with integrity and respect others. It's a small business and you need every friend you can get.

- Don't rest on your laurels, there's always something you can do to benefit your career.

WHAT VIRNA LEARNED IN YEAR FOUR

- Being well read opens you up to other possibilities; Constantly assess different ways to get what you want. And you may find you have talents for other things.

- Listen to those who have more experience than you, then do something meaningful with their advice; be willing to try new things.

- Sometimes if it feels high concept, it is high concept.

- Sometimes, you need to put everything else aside and concentrate on solely what you need to do.

- People do read your blogs and will know who you are, so be professional and respectful.

- You can have talent, connections, and an editor who loves your book and wants to buy it and still not sell. Bottom line: you need luck to sell a novel.

- There are kind people who want to help you even if they won't get anything out of it.

- When all seems lost, remind yourself and others why you're so special.

- Keep trying to make connections. Life goes on, and so will you.

- There's always a new story in me.

- Hard work doesn't always glean the results you want, but it will pay off somehow; if you persevere, people will remember you and take you seriously.

- Sometimes it's about the last man standing. Or, in this case, the last writer standing.

- Even as you celebrate one accomplishment, keep your eye on the next challenge ahead.

You May Be A Romance Writer If...

- You can't read for pleasure anymore because you end up analyzing "how" the author wrote the book.
- You're still a little confused by the black moment but would never admit it.
- Your favorite part of a story is the climax.
- You know that with some things, bigger is always better, and that smaller than six inches isn't even an option.
- You believe that people can overcome past mistakes and deserve a second chance.
- Brainstorming sessions are the equivalent of a girl's night out.
- You consistently wonder if your scenes are "hot yet tasteful."
- You actually read what you like to write.
- You find yourself working with the same Themes in your stories.
- You wonder if your agent/editor is into you.

PART IV:

IT'S YOURS FOR THE TAKING

CHAPTER 26

A LITTLE MAGIC[23]:

DESPITE THE DIFFICULTIES, IT CAN HAPPEN

Okay, so you know writing is hard. You know getting published is difficult on the best of days. But you also know you're talented and that you're talented enough to be published. Unfortunately, talent isn't always the deciding factor. Timing and luck are going to play a role, too.

Ask most successful writers and most of them will tell you it took them years to sell their first manuscript. Sometimes, the market is just so tight, you can't always break into it until one of the following four things happen:

1. You have a completed manuscript on an editor's desk when one of her regular authors can't turn her deadline books in on time.

2. A publishing house starts a new line.

3. A line is dying. (Strangely enough, this is the prime time to break in. Look around and see if a lot of authors are leaving a particular publisher and try to break in there. The caveat is, get out as soon as you can. The ship is sinking, after all.)

4. An editor changes houses.

Of course, there's always the hope that you will just write that big book, high concept, same but different novel that will knock

---

23   *A Little Magic* by Nora Roberts

an agent or an editor over. The only way to do that is to *keep writing*.

According to Lori Wilde, "All you can do is keep improving and watch what's going on around you. Get as many books out there circulating as you can. It's simply a numbers game."

Also, don't forget that you are not just a writer, but a friend, parent, partner, humanitarian, etc. You need to take care of all those parts of you. Skimping in any one area will inevitably affect your muse, too.

NETWORKING: BUILDING BRIDGES

Every year, before the RWA National conference, the same buzzword starts, well, buzzing.

Networking.

What is it, how do you do it, and why is it important?

The most basic definition of networking is building bridges. This means meeting people and creating connections. This can be done at conferences, both national and local. Networking is done at chapter meetings, both in person and online. It's done via list-serves, forums, and social networking. Networking opportunities are available every time you walk into a bookstore, or talk to another author or someone who reads books.

One of the best networking questions Tawny ever heard asked was via Kay Lockner in a workshop she'd offered on career planning. She asked the simple question "What impression do you want to make?" Then she broke it down further by specifically asking "What impression do you want to make with: 1) industry professionals; 2) other authors; and 3) readers.

Do you want to be seen as the fun gal in the bar? The consummate expert? The quiet, agreeable writer who gets things done?

When editors, agents and writers leave a conference, how do you want them to remember you? And does the impression you'd like to make fit the person you actually are?

Here's Tawny's take on the standard networking advice:

BUSINESS CARDS ARE MANDATORY AT ANY CONFERENCE OR WORKSHOP!

Business cards are nice. They should include your name, digital contact information (email, website and any social networking addresses – not a home address) and your author tagline.   After they sell their first book, many people hand out bookmarks instead of business cards.   You tend to meet a lot of people at conference, so make notes on the back of a business card to remind yourself who you met and what you discussed.

YOU HAVE TO DRESS "BUSINESS CASUAL."

It's more important that you dress like yourself. No, this doesn't mean you wear the comfy sweatpants or baggy t-shirt most writers consider our standard uniform. Instead, you want to wear professional clothes that don't make you feel like you're playing dress-up. And with that in mind, unless you're attending a themed event, dressing up in costume rarely makes a professional impression.

HAVE YOUR PITCH READY.

There's nothing more disappointing than finding yourself face to face with someone you'd like to impress and, when she asks what you write, you come up blank. Or worse, you stutter and sidestep the question. A simple two or three-sentence summary of your book or your writing is always a good thing to have memorized. It's an easy conversation opener.

NEVER SIT WITH FRIENDS AT CONFERENCE.

This is probably the one rule that I just can't get behind. I've seen how painful it is for shy people to force themselves to sit down at a table of complete strangers. If it hurts, it's not good networking. Discomfort doesn't scream "let's chat," it says "let me out of here."   On the opposite end of the spectrum is the person who grabs that last empty chair or squeezes into the seat at the lounge to be part of a group she doesn't know. Remember that for some people, conference is the only time they see writing partners or friends. Or it's their time to meet with their agents and editors. As such, they might be a little protective of that time and space. Before you sit down and interrupt, take a look at body language. By the same token, if someone does try to join you and it's not a good time, letting them know in a polite, friendly way will make everyone feel better than a rude brush-off.

DON'T STALK EDITORS OR AGENTS.

Please, please don't. They remember these things and not in a good way. Those stories you hear about people slipping their manuscript under the bathroom stall? They really happen. And it leaves the same impression a stalker would. It's creepy. The only acceptable stalking is through official channels. Attend conferences or workshops where you'll meet the editors you'd like to write for. Make a good impression by being professional and friendly. Introduce yourself at an appropriate time and hopefully they'll ask you what you write. Enter contests they're judging. Make a good impression with your entry.

YOU HAVE TO HAVE AN ONLINE PRESENCE.

More and more books are sold via the Internet. Many agents and editors research authors to see what kind of website, blog, or social media presence they have. Websites and blogs are an excellent way for readers and potential readers to find an author. Social networks can create name recognition and reader awareness. As with all networking tools, online venues create an impression – but remember, once something's online, it tends to stay there forever, and the same is true for the impression you make on others. Use your website and/or blog to promote yourself as an author, but always remember that question from earlier: What impression do you want people to have when they visit your site?

Do you want them to remember your books and writing? Then create an Internet presence that reflects the writing image you have.

Write sexy? Puppies and daisies on a website probably don't convey that message.

Write inspirational? A collection of muscle car pictures and sexy guys might bring in a lot of visitors, but unless those cars are somehow featured in your books, they may create confusion about your writing. That's not to say your website can't reflect your hobbies or interests outside of writing, but keep it in perspective. First and foremost, you're selling books, right?

ALWAYS REMEMBER TO BE POLITE.

"Please" and "thank you" go a long way. A thank you note is remembered, whether it's a thank you to an editor for a thoughtfully detailed rejection letter or to a contest judge who took the time to offer feedback and insights.

IT'S A SMALL INDUSTRY.

The romance industry might seem huge, but it's actually a very small fishbowl in a lot of ways. Word gets out. People talk. Not only about good impressions, but about bad behavior. Saying ugly things about another author while standing in line for coffee at conference tends to get back to the author. I've seen the traffic and talk generated by blogs that trash editors and agents, and by writers who identify these industry professions as being "stupid" for rejecting their "wonderful" stories. Word of these blogs and diatribes get back to editors, and even if they aren't the ones being eviscerated, they rarely want to work with someone who creates that kind of controversy. And like any small industry, the illusion of anonymity is just that – an illusion.

Just remember, there are good forms of networking and bad forms of networking.

Good networking leaves people with a positive impression of you. Bad networking, at best, makes people want to forget you. At worst it can ruin your reputation, get back to editors and agents, and negatively impact your book sales.

ACHIEVING YOUR WRITING GOALS BY NURTURING YOUR ENTIRE BEING

Writing is both an intellectual and physical pursuit. It takes stamina to sit behind a computer for hours on end and it takes a healthy body to be able to then get up and go through the motions of the rest of our lives. Being the healthiest we can be enables us to attempt more, adapt more, and accomplish more.

So, how can we achieve health in body, mind, and spirit? How can we insure that even as we pursue our passion for writing and our goal of publication that we take care of ourselves, those we love, and the other priorities in our lives?

According to Jean Marinovich, co-founder of Glycogirls, we must treat our body as an ally instead of an enemy. We do this by giving our body what it needs to thrive, and by gratefully accepting what it gives in return: a beautiful and balanced life. There are six factors that universally appear to promote health or diminish health when any one of the six factors is missing.

NUTRITION

Most often, our bodies cannot operate at optimum because they are deficient in the nutrients they need--vitamins, minerals, fatty acids and proteins. A healthy diet consists of ample fruits and vegetables, protein, good fats, and whole grains. Simple carbohydrates, such as white flour, white rice and sugar, should be limited.

Some people may need extra supplementation to target additional health issues. It's always a good idea to check with a health professional before taking supplements.

EXERCISE

Regular exercise is a necessary part of a healthy body and lifestyle because it aids every single body system. It builds muscle, which burns fat and takes pressure off over-used back muscles and protects joints. It increases bone density and decreases injury. It increases lung capacity and the transfer of oxygen in the blood. It strengthens the heart. It reduces stress and increases feel-good chemicals. Some mental health care providers prescribe exercise for depression.

Experts recommend a total of 30 to 60 minutes a day of exercise (yes, walking counts!) for optimal health. The time can be broken down into smaller increments throughout the day. A recent study showed that the body needs 450 minutes of exercise a week to maintain its weight – more to lose weight.

SLEEP

The lack of sleep, especially over time, will cause physical exhaustion, mental distraction and emotional instability. Studies show our bodies use deep sleep time to re-balance hormones and chemicals, to heal injuries and illness, and to process emotions. In addition, the body lowers cortisol levels, allowing cell growth and repair, and increases melatonin release, which fights against abnormal cell growth. When we miss sleep, these functions do not take place and our immune system is compromised.

What can cause lack of sleep? It can be caused by anxiety, exercising too close to bedtime, sluggish metabolism, dehydration, a vitamin deficiency or hormone imbalance. Consider analyzing your stress level and find ways to change situations that cause you anxiety. Next, make sure you eat healthy foods throughout the day to keep your metabolism running properly. Make sure you drink plenty of water to stay hydrated. Under a doctor's supervision, you may decide to take supplements to ensure your body is getting the vitamins and minerals it needs. In addition to a multivitamin, consider whether you want to take an extra B-vitamins supplement. Lack of vitamin Bs may contribute to increased anxiety.

In addition, think about using your bed only for sleep (oh, you know what we mean!). Reading or watching television can interfere with the brain trigger that bed equals sleep time. Create some relaxation rituals before going to bed. Taking a hot bath, meditation, or listening to soothing music may all foster sleep.

Finally, for chronic sleep problems, consider seeing a good doctor to discuss your symptoms and general health. Have your hormone levels checked, including your thyroid. Thyroid imbalances may cause a sluggish metabolism, which in turn affects sleep.

STRESS REDUCTION

What causes stress? Frustration with not being able to sell a book? Deadlines? A serious problem in a relationship? Financial pressure? Whatever it may be, stress wreaks havoc on our systems. Remember that sometimes it's not external factors that causes us stress, but how we feel about the external factor.

In order to de-stress, do what brings peace and joy; avoid what causes anxiety and pain. Easier said than done, right? Of course it is. Maybe it makes more sense to say this:

Assess the circumstances of your life and identify the key points of stress. Next, determine realistically what you can change and make a plan, enlisting trusted friends and family for support. Accept the things you cannot change with grace, fortitude, and (if possible) humor. Finally, schedule time to do things that feed your soul, be it gardening, writing, or traveling.

CONNECTION

Even those of us who cherish solitude need to connect with others. In particular, as writers, we want to feel that we can touch others' lives in some way. People with a strong network of friends and family weather struggles better and rebound quicker from setbacks. Strong support systems help us feel happy and optimistic, which in turn supports our health.

If you are feeling disconnected, reach out. Invite a friend out to a museum or to grab a cup of coffee. Ask a coworker to go for a walk in the park. Drop in on your parents or siblings. Call an old friend with whom you've lost touch. You might be surprised how appreciative of your efforts they will be. Chances are, they'd welcome the connection, too.

PASSION

The happiest people are those living their lives with passion. These people look forward to each day because they are excited about the time they are going to spend nurturing that passion.

If you're reading this book, you probably have one huge passion in your life—writing! In fact, we'd venture to say you have many more passions because like myself, the writers we've met tend to be creative in many different ways. Unfortunately, having a passion is not enough by itself to promote health. We must make our passion a priority and spend enough time following our passion to feed our souls.

Our bodies need food, our hearts need people, our minds need stimulation, and our souls need passion. When we have all of these things, we are living a life of authenticity—one that is true to ourselves. We are unfettered, unbound, unencumbered, so that even in the midst of a life full of responsibilities and giving to others, we can give to ourselves and take the time to create new characters, new worlds, and new stories.

CONCLUSION

This book has covered a lot because writing a novel involves a lot. A lot of dedication. A lot of knowledge. A lot of talent.

Our goal was to share our knowledge with you and at the same time acknowledge there's far more knowledge (and probably conflicting knowledge, at that) out there. The dedication and talent, you'll have to supply yourself. In the end, your journey is just that—yours and yours alone. Others may influence you, guide you, support you in hard times and celebrate with you during the good ones, but you determine the speed, intensity, and distance you're going to travel. Be true to yourself and your voice, and trust your instincts.

We hope that, while you pursue your writing dreams, you also strive for balance and joy in your life as a whole. If anything in this book helps you achieve that, we'll be satisfied!

There's a bumper sticker that reads: "Dance with reckless abandon." Some people reveal their passion through dance. Others reveal it through singing or painting or cooking. Heck, the lucky ones can be passionate in their every day lives.

If writing is your passion, abandon yourself to it. No matter what, get the story down. Create your world and your characters and ignore anything that gets in your way.

APPENDIX

1. FORMS YOU MAY FIND USEFUL

(Download forms at www.lovewritingbook.com in order to fill out with your own information)

TITLE:	
BASIC INFORMATION YOU NEED TO NAIL DOWN:	
GENRE:	
TAGLINE:	
LOG LINE	
HIGH CONCEPT PITCH:	
THEMATIC MESSAGE:	
SHORT THEME:	
BRAINSTORM 50 WORDS:	
SHORT OPPOSING THEME:	

BRAINSTORM 50 WORDS:	
MOTIF/SYMBOLISM:	
PREMISE HERO:	
PREMISE HEROINE:	
CHARACTER LIST:	
MAIN CHARACTERS	
PROTAGONIST:	
REMAINING HERO/HEROINE:	
EXTERNAL ANTAGONIST:	
EXTERNAL ANTAGONIST 2:	

SECONDARY MAIN CHARACTERS & THEIR PURPOSE	
If additional rows needed, place cursor in last row typed, select Table – Insert – Row Below from main toolbar.	

FLESHING OUT EACH CHARACTER AND BRAINSTORMING PLOT POINTS:	
CHARACTER:	
NAME:	
OCCUPATION:	
PHYSICAL DESCRIPTION:	
PREMISE:	
BACK STORY:	

INCORRECT CORE BELIEFS ABOUT HOW THE WORLD OPERATES:	
MASK (IDENTITY) OR HOW ACTS AS A RESULT OF ICB:	
WHAT MAKES CHARACTER SYMPATHETIC:	
WHAT MAKES CHARACTER UNIQUE:	
QUIRK 1	
QUIRK 2	
QUIRK 3	
WHAT CAN THE CHARACTER DO TO MAKE SEEM REDEEMABLE:	
FLAWS:	
Secret Wish	
Secret Fear	
Brainstorm ways characters or situations can take your character's behaviors/mask/Iden tity and grind them in his/her face (in other words challenge or	

make the character uncomfortable)	
Brainstorm what your character's Ordinary World looks like	
Brainstorm series of events that lead character to beginning of your story (Inciting Incident)	
Brainstorm where you want your character to start and where you want him/her to end (in terms of their world, their life, their personal beliefs, their outlook on life, etc)	
Brainstorm What Your Character's Initial Goal Is	
Main Character Points/Personality Traits to reveal in POV and Dialogue (Essence—Who Your Character Really Is)	
Brainstorm things that can get in the way of your character getting to the end of his/her journey and	

how they can deal with it	

A FILL-IN-THE-BLANKS FORM TO WALK YOUR CHARACTERS THROUGH THE THREE ACT STRUCTURE, INCLUDING INTERNAL, ROMANTIC, EXTERNAL CONFLICT AND CHARACTER ARC

ACT I:

_____ is the HERO OR HEROINE of the story. Physical description: _____

Character notes: _____

GIVING your character INTERNAL CONFLICT

Because of how your character grew up or what your character experienced _____, your character has the following flawed views about the world/other people/his or her own value or worth: _____.   What your character secretly fears most is_____. As such, because of these flawed views and fears, your character acts like this on the outside: _____. On the inside, your character is really like this: _____. What your character secretly/really wants most is: _____.   However, at this time your character is not willing to change/act to get it.

STAGE 1: SET UP/VIEW INTO THE PROTAGONIST'S ORDINARY WORLD

At the very beginning of the story, his/her ordinary world looks like _____.

Whether your character knows it or not, several things in his/her world need fixing, including _____. However, because your character is not willing to face his/her fears yet and because your character still carries the shadows of his/her past, your character THINKS your character wants this out of life: _____.

Turing Point 1: (OPPORTUNITY FORCES CHARACTER INTO ACTION AND STARTS CONFLICT)

Then _____ (the Inciting Incident) happens and gets in the way of his/her initial goal. This forces him/her to adopt an external goal, _____. His/her initial plan to achieve the goal is _____. His/her motivation is _____.

STAGE 2: PROGRESS

This is what your character does to achieve the goal: _____. What other stuff can be happening at this time? _____

Turning Point 2: (SOMETHING UNEXPECTED HAPPENS, LIKELY THE FIRST DEFEAT, RESULTS IN CHANGE OF PLANS OR GOAL)

Whatever your character is doing to get his/her goal causes problems for the ANTAGONIST because: _____. This is how the ANTAGONIST responds: _____. Of course, this in turn causes problems for your character. How? _____. As a result, your character has this realization _____ and decides to modify his/her plans by doing _____ in order to achieve his/her goal. This forces (your character) to grow a little by _____ or his/her refusal to grow affects him or her this way: _____. What other stuff can be happening at this time? _____

MAKING SURE YOU HAVE ROMANTIC AND INTERAL CONFLICT, TOO. WEAVE THE FOLLOWING INTO YOUR STORY AS THE EXTERNAL PLOT PROGRESSES:

In the meantime, HERO AND HEROINE meet when _____. They are attracted to one another. However, HERO AND HEROINE'S ROMANTIC CONFLICTS (which are _____ and _____) cause them to pull away or resist one another.

Nonetheless, because of _____ they must still be around one another. Use your answers at the very beginning to show your character acting consistently with his incorrect core beliefs/fears while still making sure you hint at who your character really is. How can your characters challenge or exploit your character's fears and incorrect core beliefs? _____ How could your character respond? _____

ACT II:

STAGE 3: INCREASED COMPLICATIONS

Despite (or because of) obstacles caused by the ANTAGONIST, your character's goal at this point is _____. His/her plan to achieve the goal is

_____. His/her motivation is _____. This is what your character does to achieve the goal: _____. This also happens: _____. In the meantime, your character's actions _____ cause problems for ANTAGONIST who responds by _____. Of course, this in turn causes problems for your character because _____. Repeat Stage 3 if necessary. What other stuff can be happening at this time? _____

MAKING SURE YOU'RE STILL WEAVING IN INTERNAL AND ROMANTIC CONFLICT:

At the same time, HERO AND HEROINE are still attracted to one another.

Unfortunately, this _____ still keeps them apart. Despite this, they still manage to get closer when _____. Invariably, your character begins to reveal more and more of who your character really is on the inside by: _____. However, because your character is still mistrustful/scared, your character continues to act out on his/her flawed views and fears by: _____. How can your characters challenge or exploit your character's fears and incorrect core beliefs? _____ How could your character respond? _____

Turning Point 3: (GREATER SETBACK RESULTS IN CHARACTER'S FULL COMMITMENT AND TO POINT OF NO RETURN)

Despite (or because of) obstacles caused by the ANTAGONIST, your character's goal at this point is _____. His/her plan to achieve the goal is _____. His/her motivation is _____. This is what your character does to achieve the goal: _____. This also happens: _____. Your character's actions _____ cause problems for ANTAGONIST who responds by _____. Of course, this in turn causes problems for your character because _____. As a result of this, as well as his/her contact with the hero/heroine, your character has this realization _____ and decides to modify his/her plans by doing _____ in order to achieve her goal. This forces (your character) to grow by _____. Your character is now fully committed to his goal and there is no going back. However, this change is not permanent and will be tested one more time at the black moment (below). How can your characters challenge or exploit your character's fears and incorrect core beliefs? _____. How could your character respond? _____. What other stuff can be happening at this time? _____

STAGE 4: FINAL PUSH; PROTAGONIST APPEARS TO BE LOSING

Despite (or because of) obstacles caused by the ANTAGONIST, your Character's goal is _____. His/her plan to achieve the goal is _____. His/her motivation is _____. This is what your character does to achieve the goal: _____. This also happens: _____. your character's actions _____ cause problems for ANTAGONIST who responds by _____. Of course, this in turn causes problems for your character because _____. Things are looking very bad for your character here.

MAKING SURE YOU'RE STILL WEAVING IN INTERNAL AND ROMANTIC CONFLICT:

As things are getting worse in terms of the external plot, your character is pushed more and more to reveal who your character really is to the love interest. Your character does this by _____. The hero and heroine grow emotionally closer, each recognizing their growing feelings, even if your character is not willing to express it or fully commit. How can your characters challenge or exploit your character's fears and incorrect core beliefs? _____ How could your character respond? _____

Turning Point 4: (MAJOR SET BACK THAT RESULTS IN THE BLACK MOMENT)

Despite your character's best effort to achieve his/her goal, things get steadily worse because _____. Although your character does this _____, the ANTAGONIST responds by _____, gaining an advantage. The reader now believes that all is lost for your character because _____. What other stuff can be happening at this time? _____

MAKING SURE YOU'RE STILL WEAVING IN INTERNAL AND ROMANTIC CONFLICT:

Moreover, things are about to implode in the romantic plot. This happens: _____. This is your character's worst fear because: _____ and he/se retreats back into himself/herself one last time, showing your character has not achieved the full growth that your character needs to. Your character reverts to his flawed views and fears and does this _____. This separates him/her from the love interest how? _____

ACT III:

STAGE 5: REALIZATION/AFTERMATH

After the your character is separated after the black moment, this happens: _____your character has the following realization: _____. With this realization, your character is finally willing to risk it all to achieve his/her goal and/or show his true love for. What other stuff can be happening at this time? _____

Turning Point 5: (CLIMAX)

As a result of his/her realization, your character decides to do _____, which places him head to head with ANTAGONIST. This is what happens: _____.

STAGE 6: RESOLUTION

As a result of achieving his/her full character growth, your character achieves _____. Whereas your character started out like this _____, your character has become _____. Even his/her world has changed in this way: _____. How has solving their romantic conflict changed their lives? _____

2. A GREAT AND TERRIBLE BEAUTY[24]:

HONEST ANSWERS TO FAQS (AND SOME QUESTIONS WE WISHED WE'D ASKED EARLIER)

GETTING STARTED

What software do most writers use and what are some valuable software tips?

Most writers use some version of Microsoft Word. However, writers also use writing programs such as Scrivener, Power Structure, WriteItNow or Storyist. The reasons authors might use these programs are project management, organization, or viewing options. Many programs allow you to see your chapters and scenes as virtual index cards in a storyboard or corkboard. See www.vanessakier.com for articles on writing technology.

What's Romance Writers of America and should I join?

It is a national organization formed to support romance writers and create positive exposure for the romance genre in general. The amount of information, insights and support it provides can be an invaluable boon on the ups and downs of your publishing journey.

How do I find a critique partner? How do I know when someone is a good fit for me?

Critique partners can be found in person and online. Many RWA chapters (again, local and online) have critique groups or programs. Other sources are writing groups, bookstores and literacy programs. The best way to make sure your experience is a good one is to take it a single step at a time. Make sure you have a rapport with the other person before sharing your soul--or

---

24   *A Great And Terrible Beauty* by Libba Bray

in this case, your story. Agree to critique a single scene or chapter to see how it goes.

What's the best way to write a novel?

There's no one way to write a novel. Honestly, the best advice Virna ever got was to sit down and write the story that was in her head. She started with a general concept and characters – a buttoned-up female prosecutor with a hidden, dark past that makes her the worst partner for the hero, a defense attorney she's worked with before.

The best way, Tawny believes, is whatever way gets it written. For all the tips and processes we've included here, the reality is that there are, to quote Jennifer Crusie, "Many Roads to Oz." In other words, there is no single way to write. No one process that's better than the other. The key is to keep trying out new things until you find the one, or ones, that work for you.

What's the process for getting a book published by a traditional publisher?

Generally, you write and polish your manuscript. Then you query agents until you get representation. Then your agent submits your manuscript to editors until one makes an offer. Of course, there are ways to vary from this process. You can pitch to an agent or editor and get them interested in you and your story that way. The agent or editor might request some pages, and ask for more if they're interested. (Not to burst your bubble, but it's a reality that sometimes agents or editors routinely request pages from everyone who pitches to them; this, however, is not always true!) They might ask you to revise or submit something else. Or they might pass. The important thing to remember is that an agent or editor is going to be focused on a specific work, not on your potential to be a great writer or to have a great platform. In general, those things will be considered, but most of the time the agent and editor is looking for a manuscript they can sell with very little tweaking needed. The time for agents and editors to "grow" writers by working them over a lengthy period of time is a bit of a myth nowadays.

MISCONCEPTIONS

Isn't getting published all about who's the best writer?

No, it's all about the marketability of the book. Sometimes the most marketable books are produced by the "best" writers, but sometimes they are not. Who is the "best" is also subject to debate. Agents, editors, and readers will not always agree on what makes for the best writer or story.

Selling a novel will validate my writing talent, right?

It might do so for a very brief time, but it shouldn't. Just because you were published over someone else doesn't necessarily mean you are a better writer. If you haven't sold your novel, that doesn't mean you aren't a great writer, either. And the unfortunate truth is, being published brings its own set of challenges--reviews, reader feedback, second book syndrome. So really, the best validation should come from your own faith in your talent.

Aren't all romances published by Harlequin?

No. Harlequin publishes both single title and category lines, but many publishers also publish romance.

To increase my chances of getting published, shouldn't I write whatever genre is "hot" at the moment?

This is up for debate. People will often tell you not to write for the market because then your lack of enthusiasm for your story will be obvious. Virna doesn't necessarily agree with this.

The first two books she sold were the result of a conscious effort on her part to write what was "hot," i.e., paranormal romance. That said, she also came up with a story idea she was jazzed about. Plus, when she wrote the story, she felt an immediate affinity and enthusiasm for it. This was partly because she loved reading paranormal romances, but also because she chose to write a paranormal romantic suspense. In essence, she wrote a story similar to what she'd already loved writing (romantic suspense). She was just open to adding another element to it, the paranormal element, because she felt it would increase her chances of selling.

An agent/editor just requested my full manuscript. I'm close to representation or a sale, right?

Not necessarily. What it means is that an agent or editor sees the potential in the pages he/she has already read and wants to read more. Of course, it's a good sign, but don't be surprised if that same agent or editor ultimately passes. Also keep in mind that if the agent or editor passes, but has suggestions, take those suggestions seriously. They wouldn't spend time detailing what worked or didn't work unless they felt the work had serious potential. If you get a request, submit it. If they ask for revisions, strongly consider making the changes (as long as they fit your vision of your story) and resubmit.

Everyone is writing a novel so why should I even try?

First, why wouldn't you do something you think you'll enjoy? Who cares how many other people are doing it? Second, if you mean you want to be published and there are many people writing a novel (meaning, there's a lot of competition out there), same answer. Also, a lot of people want to write a novel or say they are writing a novel, but they aren't seriously doing it.

According to the statistics, if I think positively, I'll get published.

Not necessarily, but positive thinking helps because it will keep you going, and truly, perseverance is what is going to get you published. One of the basic tenets of thinking positively, or The Law of Attraction, is that you not only keep a great, upbeat attitude but do whatever you can to get yourself published. Write, get feedback. Submit. Write more, submit more. Keep working toward publication and that, as well as your positive attitude, will go a long way toward getting you published.

If I work hard, I'll get published.

Hard work will go a long way toward achieving your publishing goals. But, unfortunately there are never any guarantees in this business.

WRITING CRAFT

What are the most well-known "rules" about writing?

Don't head hop. Don't use a lot of adverbs (-ly words). Write in active voice. Vary sentence structure. Write with equal amounts action, dialogue, and narrative. Avoid huge chunks of exposition in back story or info dumps. According to J.A. Konrath, some ways to avoid this are to break the info into small snippets of dialogue; break it up with conflict; put in less info by trusting your reader more and letting them make logical connections; make readers wait for information, which creates tension, and keep it brief. In addition, remember that white space, which is common with dialogue, is reader friendly.

Should I write a prologue?

It depends. There are differing views on this. As addressed above, people disagree about where to start a novel. Jenny Crusie says the first page starts with the trouble and the conflict needs to be established by the end of the first scene. She advocates showing what people are doing now, and that a writer should assume the reader knows back story. As for prologues, Jennifer Crusie hates them. Lori Wilde believes it is better not to have a prologue if you can skip it, but that sometimes they serve a purpose. Likewise, Mary Buckham advises that prologues be compelling and not just a tool for dumping in back story (commonly called an "information dump" or "back story dump").

What does "saving the cat" mean?

This is a term coined by the late screenwriter Blake Snyder, who wrote a craft book called "Save The Cat." It means to give your characters, especially your protagonist, a likable quality that hints at the fact that they are redeemable. In other words, if your character is a bit on the edge in terms of likeability, showing him doing something like saving a cat will make the reader relate to him more.

In the writing context, what's the difference between "Alpha" and "Beta?"

These terms describe personality traits, typically those of males. An Alpha always thinks they know best, are assured and take charge. Typical Alphas are cops, military and CEOs. Betas are mellower. They are often the best friend, the charmer, the intellectual. And then there are Gammas, that wonderful combination of Alpha and Beta, a character who is usually Beta, but gets very Alpha in special circumstances.

What does GMC mean and why does everyone keep talking about it?

It means Goal, Motivation, & Conflict. A popular writing book was written by Deb Dixon on these subjects. Goal, motivation and conflict are great characterization tools that help establish who the characters are, what they want (usually an external, conscious goal), what their fears and issues are (Internal Conflict), what they really want out of life (story goal) and what stands in their way (External Conflict).

Do I have to introduce my protagonist first in the story?

Some authors believe that protagonist should be introduced on the first page of a story so the reader becomes invested in the character. They might say that when the villain is introduced first, you risk placing the reader's focus on him rather than the protagonist. As such, introduce the protagonist, his problem and his goal and either foreshadow the antagonist or have him with the protagonist.

There are other opinions about this, however. For example, although a creepy prologue can put off some readers, it puts up front what your book is about and gives the reader the right to opt out. In addition, the killer/stalker antagonist in a prologue is a popular device because it's effective. If you do it, try to put a twist on it so it's fresh.

Can I have more than one antagonist?

Some people believe that having more than one antagonist dilutes the conflict and thus the ultimate catharsis for the reader.

However, others have no problem with having more than one antagonist. In addition, you can have one major antagonist, and smaller villains who are agents for the antagonist.

Finally, as we've detailed above, a story generally has three antagonists anyway—the external antagonist, the internal antagonist (the character's internal conflict resulting from back story/Incorrect Core Beliefs), and the romantic antagonist (the romantic interest and all the baggage he/she brings to the table to interact with the other character's).

How flawed can I make my main characters?

A perfect character is hard for readers to relate to. Perfection leaves no room for growth, so perfect characters are hard for writers to write, as well. Characters need flaws.

How flawed?

As much as your story requires, as long as it fits your story's tone and Theme. Often times, especially for romance readers, it's better if a hero or heroine's "sins" aren't shown on the page. For instance saying that the hero sold a little pot in the past is a little different than showing him doing it. In other ways, it might be a case of knowing when to show and when to tell.

WRITING BUSINESS

What is a "stock signing?"

When an author goes into a bookstore and asks to sign the books the bookstore has "in stock." Autographed books sell well, plus if they are signed it potentially limits the ability of the bookstore to return them. Stock signings can also be done at any other store that carries books. Targets, Walmarts, etc...

Do I have to write a whole book in order to sell it?

Usually. If you're unpublished, probably. If you've been published before, it depends.

Do I have to be outgoing to be a successful author?

Not necessarily, but what's your definition of successful? Writers generally write to an audience. To find your audience, you might have to put yourself "out there." It's usually easier to start with people you have something in common with—like other writers. You'll get encouragement and support and probably meet potential readers through them.

I read so many "bad" books, so how come I can't get published?

Always remember that writing is subjective. That "bad" book was published because multiple industry professional felt it met the needs of the market at the time it was bought and published.

How will I know if my agent or editor is "into me?"

If they get back to you when you email or call them in a reasonable amount of time (and a reasonable amount of time is always going to be more time than you'd like). If they listen to you, respond appropriately, and make time for you when it really matters. If they keep reading or buying your manuscripts.

What's the Golden Heart and should I enter it?

The Golden Heart is RWA's national unpublished contest. The entries consist of 50 pages and are judged by members of RWA with a simple scoring of 1 through 9. There is no feedback, though, so really the only goal of entering the contest is to final. Finaling is a big deal. These full manuscripts are then sent to acquiring editors for final judging. The finalists are featured on the RWA website, they have a champagne reception at the National Conference and are honored in a fancy award ceremony where the winners are announced.

What's the Rita and should I enter it?

The Rita is the published author's equivalent of the Golden Heart, but instead of the first 50 pages being judged, the entire book is judged.

What's RWA National Conference like? Is it important to go?

Virna: I've been to a few and have enjoyed every one. At some point, though, I get overwhelmed by how many people are there and go to my room for a little alone time. My first National, I skipped all the group meals because I was so overwhelmed. But I attended every one after that. I love mingling with other writers, getting to take workshops, and in general getting inspired to write again.

How important is it to pitch to an agent and editor at conference?

Virna: I think it's important because it gives you practice talking about your story. Although it can be nerve-racking, once it's done, you generally will realize that agents and editors are "regular" people who want the people who pitch to them to feel comfortable. I always think that giving them a "face" to connect to a name puts you one step above those manuscripts that are in the slush pile.

Don't I want a five-book deal if possible?

A multi-book deal sounds great, doesn't it? It provides security, a chance to build a readership, long-term work. The downside to a multi-book contract is that you're tied to a particular storyline and publishing contract for a year or two (or five). For example, what if you end up being hugely popular from the get go? What incentive does the publishing house have to give you more money when they've already contracted with you for a certain (and probably much smaller) advance? Many houses' multi-book contracts contain pitfalls to watch out for, as well. Have a good agent both negotiate and explain the terms.

What is a "proposal?"

A synopsis and the first three chapters of an author's work.

What is a "blog" and should I do one?

A blog –or web log- is similar to an online journal for some, a mini-magazine for others. Blog posts run the range of weekly musings, book reviews or mini articles. Many authors have personal blogs, or join with other authors in group blogs in order to promote their work and keep their name active on the web.

What are the most well-known "rules" about publishing?

Don't slide your manuscript under the bathroom stall to an editor or agent. Seriously. Keep your submissions professional – no glitter or rainbow paper.

Should I Twitter? Facebook? MySpace?

These are all social networks that can be accessed on the Internet. The idea is to grow your presence so more people know about you and your books. You gather followers on Twitter, friends on Facebook, and followers on MySpace. If you have the time and the inclination, why not?

Should I design a trailer for my book?

The benefit of having a professional trailer is in having something else you can use to promote yourself on bookseller sites. Again, if you have the time and the inclination (and money or talent to make one), why not?

I hear the publishers give away free books at RWA National Conference. Who gets them?

Anyone who is registered for the national conference can attend the publisher giveaways. There's some debate whether you need to wait in line with the people waiting to get their books signed by the author or, if you're not interested in getting a signed copy, you can just walk up to the table and grab one.

PERSONAL NOTE FROM TAWNY: Oh please, don't cut in line. Cutting ahead to grab a book means that the people who are excited and love that author enough to wait in line for an autograph might be shortchanged once they get up front and the books are gone.

What is a "brand" or "platform?"

A platform is most often used in non-fiction to describe the message the author is focusing on. In a way, it's the author's resume –what do they bring to the table to make them an expert? What's their skill or talent or connections that will carry the book sales and help get the message out to readers? An author's platform is the way you reach readers. It's a network and it's notoriety. It's exposure.

The word "brand" is used to refer to a product or company name or anything unique that identifies something using a logo or trademark. An author brand builds an image or identity that is used to create "emotional Velcro"--a perception of something special that is of higher quality.

Example: "Do you have the latest Nora book?," which refers to Nora Roberts's author "brand."

Should I use a pen name?

Is your name difficult to spell? Would it keep readers from finding you on the web or in bookstores? Do you want to keep your real name saved for a particular type of book you'll be writing in the future? For example, if you are writing erotica but know you'll eventually want to write thrillers, do you want to use your real name for both? Or will you want to use a pen name for the eroticas and your real name for the thrillers?   Are you concerned with anonymity/privacy. One thing to consider is that your real name is generally printed on a book's copyright page.

What is an RWA PRO member and why should I be one?

An RWA PRO is an RWA member who has completed a full manuscript and submitted that manuscript to an agent or editor. The benefit of becoming a PRO is that RWA has specific resources set aside for PROs—PRO loops, PRO specific workshops at national conference. PROs also get priority over non PRO members when signing up for pitch appointments for national conference.

What is an RWA PAN member and why should I be one?

Any RWA member who has earned at least $1,000 on a single book through either an advance, royalties, or a combination of the two. Just like PRO members, they receive certain benefits from RWA, such as PAN specific loops and workshops.

What is a vanity press?

A vanity press or vanity publisher is a publishing house that publishes books at the author's expense. However, it is expensive to publish your book through a vanity press, and most authors normally do not recoup the expense. Generally, major publishing houses will not give prior works published through a vanity press much weight.

What is a small press?

Small press is a term often used to describe publishers with annual sales below a certain level, usually $50 million. Small presses are also defined as those that publish an average of fewer than 10 titles per year.

The terms "small press", "indie publisher," and "independent press" are often used interchangeably, with "independent press" defined as publishers that are not part of large multinational corporations. Small presses often release books intended for specialized audiences.

What is an e-press?

A publisher that mainly produces books in electronic format.

Should I e-publish?

It depends on what your wants and needs are. Many authors have made successful careers with e-books. Generally, you don't get paid an advance but get a royalty rate on the exact number of books sold.

Author Elle Amery writes for the e-press, Ravenous Romance. She believes there are both pros and cons to e-publishing. The pros are 1) it makes writing as a career "real" for beginning authors, which builds confidence; 2) it gives the writer an opportunity to hone her craft, as well as learn to adhere to a schedule and be responsive to an editor; in particular, with Ravenous Romance the word count is expected to be about 50,000-60,000, and in writing books with a shorter word count, the writer learns to write to "the meat" of the story; 3) e-readers are voracious and thus e-presses generate high quantities of books in a shorter time than traditional presses; Amery has published five books in a year-and-a-half with her e-press 4) e-presses are generally more willing to contract a greater number of writers, and help writers learn and build a fan base; 5) writers generally have greater freedom to cross genres; and 6) some e-presses, like Ravenous Romance, have been successful in finding traditional print publishers to buy their authors' print rights.

On the downside, Amery points to: 1) the need to produce new books very quickly (she usually is given 6-8 weeks to write her books), which means there is less time for authors to revise their work; 2) although it is possible for e-authors to make a lot of money, they often have to do a lot of self-marketing to achieve this; and 3) readers beyond a certain age do not view e-books as "real books."

Should I self-publish?

Again, it depends. Is your primary goal to see your story in "book form." Or keeping control over every aspect of it? Is it a "specialty" type book that has a limited audience and therefore would not need the wide distribution that a traditional publisher could offer? Would you enjoy hand-selling/marketing your book? Would you rather wait and see if you can make the story into something a traditional publisher might want, even knowing it might take years to make the sale? These are all things for you to consider.

Do I have to write sex to write romance?

No. You need to write romance and a happy ending. Many romance readers like reading about sex, and the steamier the better, but there are plenty of sweet romances where sex isn't a requirement. You can also write a story with romantic elements, which downplays reader expectation for sexual elements. In addition, there is a line of romances called Inspirationals that are faith based and often do not show sex on the page.

I just got a rejection. What does "not compelling enough" mean?

First, it could be that the agent or editor had a hard time pinpointing what wasn't working for her/him with the story. Often times, they just know it wasn't working. Not compelling enough can also mean the stakes and the pacing weren't high enough and the story failed to keep the reader on the edge of her seat. Think about whether your conflict is strong enough (including whether it's personal and involves high stakes) to make the reader truly care about the journey the character is taking. You might also ask whether a "ticking clock" is creating urgency in terms of passing time.

Why is being "mid-list" sometimes considered a negative thing?

A mid-list author is one that continues to produce and publish books, but without any huge "break out" success. Their readership, popularity, and advances may continue to increase in small increments, but their sell through numbers don't necessarily meet the publisher's hopes. The danger of being a mid-list author is that your publishing "slot" might be taken by an up and coming author who the publisher believes has the capability to "break out" and make the publisher more money.

What's the benefit of presenting a workshop at an RWA National Conference?

Exposure. The chance to get others to know who you are and hear what you have to say. It's not a real financial benefit, because although you get a credit towards your conference registration fee, this credit is relatively small to begin with and is split between all workshop presenters. That said, many people send workshop proposals and only a small number get accepted. Presenting a workshop is a chance for you to shine in front of your fellow authors, give back to the writing community, and let them know what you and your books are about.

What's a special interest chapter in RWA?

A special interest chapter is designed to serve members of RWA with common interests. For example, writers who write mystery or suspense, paranormal, erotica, etc.

What is the query process like?

The query process begins with identifying the agent or editor you are interested in. You should then determine whether the agent or editor prefers queries by email or snail mail. You will write a query letter and follow the guidelines set by that agent or editor. For example, some ask that you automatically send them the first 10 pages of your manuscript with your query letter. Some want only the letter. Some will ask for a synopsis. Most authors send multiple queries. You then wait to hear whether the agent or editor wants more from you or has "passed" on seeing more of your work. A pass usually comes in the form of a form rejection (one that is sent out to authors in general) but can also come in more personalized form, addressed to you and signed by the agent or editor.

Should I pay for a book doctor to help me edit my book?

The typical advice is that money should never flow from the author, but flow to the author. Sometimes, however, we are tempted to seek professional help to make our work the best it can be. If you decide to use a book doctor, speak to prior clients and be clear on what you are paying for, i.e., whether you are looking for line edits, general impressions, suggestions or brainstorming help, etc.

What is NaNoWriMo and should I do it?

National Novel Writing Month is a phenom started by Chris Baty. It challenges writers to write 50,000 words in the month of

November. The work is technically supposed to be a new one (not a work in progress) and the goal is to write forward and not worry whether what you write is "good" or not.

Should I force myself to talk to that author, agent or editor at a meeting or conference?

You shouldn't force yourself to do anything that you are very uncomfortable with, but if you want to challenge yourself to increase your networking skills, there are many benefits.

When a work has been "requested," how long do I have to submit it?

There's no hard and fast rule, but in general, within one year at the outside.

Does promotion really make a difference in getting or staying published?

Most people say they don't know. It's a very hard thing to track. However, publishers are leaning more heavily on their authors to promote, so this speaks to whether it matters or not. Name recognition does help sell books. Ask yourself whether you enjoy it, can you afford it, and do you feel like it's worth doing? Some people market like crazy, some are more laid back about it. We've seen authors who are successful in both camps.

Do bad reviews matter? Do good ones?

They matter if they're about your book and you read them, for sure. Most industry professionals agree that any press is good press. But as far as the general perception of reviews, it seems most readers don't pay much attention to them.

Should I write category if my main goal is to write single title?

Many "big" authors started out in category. It's where you can hone your craft and get professional feedback on your work and learn more about the business. Are you hoping to bring your category readers over? In general, the two audiences don't have a lot of cross over.

Despite some perceptions, category books aren't easier to write, nor are they "just short single titles." Writing for a category line is actually more difficult in many ways than writing single title because of the line requirements, the short word count and the tight pace. Many category authors, having mastered the skill of meeting these requirements, find it challenging to make the shift to single title as their voice has developed a strong "category feel."

Should I write single title if my main goal is to write category?

You need to think about why you would. Is the single title genre similar to what you would be writing in category? Are you hoping to bring your single title audience over to you when you write your categories? In general, the two audiences don't have a lot of cross over. Moreover, once you've mastered writing larger books, you'll have to learn how to write shorter ones. Writing for a category line is actually more difficult in many ways than writing single title because of the line requirements, the short word count and the tight pace.

What's high concept and how can I write a high concept book?

"High concept" is a slippery term that is defined in different ways by different people. Generally, it is a blockbuster idea, one that has a hook and twist that is broadly appealing to a larger audience. It's a film in which the director can cast any actor and have a "break out" film. According to Alexandra Sokoloff, while a log line can describe an interesting story, she maintains it is not "high concept" unless "everyone who hears it can see exactly what the movie or book is—and a majority of people who hear it will want to see it or read it..." See Chapter 18, *infra*.

What is the Brenda Novak Online Auction For Diabetes Research and how can it help me?

Brenda Novak is a bestselling author who has a son with diabetes. With her many connections in the publishing industry, she started an auction to help raise money for diabetes research.

In May 2010, she hit the $1 million dollar mark. There are plenty of prizes and networking connections to be made by those interested in writing and publishing in general. See www.brendanovak.com for more information on this worthy cause.

Why should I join a local writing chapter? Why should I volunteer to serve on its Board?

We can only speak from my experience. We've both grown tremendously as writers by being part of local writing organizations. We've met some great people and stayed motivated by sharing common experiences when things seemed bleak.

Networking isn't a requirement in this industry, but it definitely helps. Hearing what other writers are going through, what publishers are looking for, what concepts are trending are all great things. The encouragement and support chapters provide often make it well worthwhile to join.

AGENTS

Do I need an agent? How do I get one? How does an agent make money off me?

A writer can use all the help she can get. She can use every advocate in her corner. So if you can get an agent, why not get one? You don't necessarily NEED one if you feel comfortable handling contract matters on your own. However, an agent can often get an author more offers and a better deal. Agents also act as intermediaries between an author and an editor, handle subsidiary rights, and give an author advice on career goals and the state of the market.

Agents are partners for authors. They advocate their author's work, they negotiate contracts and often if they hear of ideas that would suit their author, they can open a door in a way an author can't themselves. Whether they are needed or not is always up to the individual author. If you are comfortable negotiating contracts (or would prefer to have a contract lawyer look over yours), if you've got a relationship with editors that will help you sell books, or if you're selling and doing well in an area that you don't need an agent, then one wouldn't be necessary. Agents earn money by charging a commission (generally 15%) from their author's earnings.

Once I land an agent, how long will it take me to sell?

There's no way to guarantee you will. But having an agent might help you see what isn't working and figure out a new direction to pursue if sales aren't coming together.

Once I have an agent, editors will take me seriously, right?

Hopefully, assuming you have a good agent. However, being taken more seriously doesn't necessarily mean anything in terms of increasing your chances of a sale or hearing back from editors quickly.

When a good agent wants to represent me, won't they have me sign a contract?

Not necessarily. Some agents from top-tier agencies don't have their clients sign a contract.

An agent has asked me to revise my manuscript without guaranteeing me representation. Should I do it?

Virna did it twice and it worked out well both times. That said, you need to think about where you are in your journey, what other interest you've had, and how much you want this agent. Moreover, you need to ask yourself whether you agree the revisions would make the story stronger and whether they fit your vision of the story.

What will my relationship with my agent be like?

Relationships vary, of course. The typical relationship relies primarily on email. You might see your agent at national conference or when she's near your town. Agents typically keep you apprised of submissions and forward you rejections.

EDITORS

I found an editor who loves my book so aren't I guaranteed to get published?

No. There are other factors that may result in your book not getting published. Whether the editor has the final purchasing power is a huge one. Moreover, even if your editor is the senior editor, a publisher's marketing department can also shoot a sale down.

What will my relationship with my editor be like?

Relationships vary, of course. Sometimes, especially in a new relationship, an author will just communicate with an editor via email, and only on an "as needed" basis.

FINANCES

How much money will I make if I get published?

It varies. The bigger publishing houses pay advances. E-publishers often do not pay advances (or pay very small ones), but give a higher rate on royalties.

What's the cost of doing writing business?

See Virna's cost breakdown in Chapter 25. Generally, you might have to pay for:

Membership in RWA

Membership in local writing chapters

Contests

Conferences Fees

Mailing Fees

Airfare

Hotel

Critique Services/Book Doctors

Promotion

Website

BEFORE GETTING PUBLISHED

How valuable are writing contests if I want to be published?

It depends how you target contests. Virna didn't find them particularly helpful. Although she placed second in the first contest she entered, and it was an achievement to talk about in a query letter, it didn't seem to hold as much impact as one would think. For the other contests she entered, she got inconsistent feedback, and thus wasn't sure who to believe. In the end, she found that unless she knew who was reading her entry and could respect their opinion, it wasn't very helpful to her.

Tawny, on the other hand, found contests quite useful. She finaled and won quite a few, which create a strong sense of name recognition among RWA members, as well as among the editors she'd targeted via the contests. Also, oftentimes after a manuscript has been submitted to an editor (or even rejected by an editor), writers still tweak and write and change it – a contest is a way to get those improvements in front of the editor.

Should I have a website (or market myself) before I'm published?

Yes. Both Tawny and Virna did this. By the time we sold, we had a small readership started already. People knew who we were.

I've written my manuscript. Now what?

Get feedback on it. Revise and polish it if necessary. Send it out to be read. Research where you'll submit it, polish it again, then submit.

AFTER GETTING PUBLISHED

How do I determine if my published book is selling well?

Often times the only true measure of sales is a royalty statement that will break down exactly what's sold, when and in which format. Your editor or agent should be able to get you rough numbers while you wait , as well. Bookscan reflects a portion of your numbers, but it only reflects a fraction of your sales.

Once I sell a book, how long will it be before I get my contract? Money? First book signing?

It's hard to say. For Virna: I got "the call" on November 18, 2010. I didn't sign my contract until after the new year. I didn't get my first advance check until sometime in February 2010. In addition, although I had due dates built into my contract (to turn in a revised full and a proposed full), those dates have been revised due to the publisher's time schedule. This delays when I can turn things in and thus, when I get my money as well. My first book is set to come out (and signed!) in April of 2011.

For Tawny: I got the call on May 29, 2006, and my contract arrived within the next month. I received the first half of my advance about two weeks after returning my contract. Generally speaking, I always receive my money within two weeks of it's release (it's released when my editor accepts my proposal, partial or full for publication) . My first set of author copies of my debut book arrived about 6 weeks before their release date.

Do I get input into my cover design? Book blurb?

You usually get input, but not final say. It's important to remember to let people do what they're good at. You have to trust they know what they're doing. In addition, however, it's nice to have an agent for situations like this, because your agent can act as your advocate and talk to the editor or art department and express your concerns for you.

Once I sell, do I get my money all at once?

Not usually. You will probably get it in segments. It is most typical to get an advance upon the signing of the contract, another portion at the time your revised draft is accepted, and another portion at the time your book comes out. If your contract is for more than one book, then you will also receive a segment of money when you turn in the proposal for the second book, when the revised full manuscript is accepted, and when the second book comes out.

Is being published worth all the heartache?

From Virna: I think so, but I can't say for sure yet since my book doesn't come out until April 2011. Envisioning my book on the shelf makes me believe it's all worth it. But until it's actually there? And until my next one's there? And the next one? I can't say for sure. Can anyone really answer that question definitively? I can say that getting to my first sale has been worth the heartache because I know I stayed true to my passion and didn't give up. Those are things to be proud of in my mind.

From Tawny: Oh man, yes! Totally worth it! I love writing, I love being published. There are definitely headaches and heartaches involved, but you'll face those in anything, won't you? There's nothing more amazing than seeing your book--that incredible creation you thought up, dreamed of, crafted and poured your heart into--on a bookstore shelf. It's amazing to hear from readers, to know your work touched others.

HEALTH/FAMILY/PERSONAL LIFE
Will I be "judged" for writing romance?

Some people (be it family, friends, peers, reviewers, etc) are certain to judge you because they will have preconceptions about how "easy" it is to write a romance or to get published. Others will view writing as a hobby or a pipe dream, somehow less validating than "real" work. Still others will belittle the value of romance books in general, comparing it to "soft porn" or formulaic trash. The good news is you know better, romance readers are amazingly loyal and voracious, and others will see writing as an exotic, mysterious, and gutsy career choice. That said, try not to take things personally and try not to have a thin skin. No one likes to be judged and some people just want to knock you down—don't let them.

How can I avoid gaining weight as I write?

Watch what you eat and exercise. Find other stress releases than food (we recommend exercise). Make sure you get up and move around during those hours you spend in front of the computer. Sorry, we know it's a lot easier said than done.

What do I do if my friends/husband/family doesn't support my writing?

Find people who do support you, especially other writers. By attending writing conferences and chapter meetings, you can get information but also inspiration. Inevitably, you'll find many others struggle with the same issues and challenges you do. You might also get some tips on how to handle them.

How can I stay emotionally healthy despite the constant ups and downs of the publishing business?

Don't take things personally. Don't seek to validate yourself through your writing. Don't question your talent or destiny if you meet obstacles. You might question your methods, but seek objective opinions on this, as well.

3. GLOSSARY

- ACT – a thing done; a main division of play, ballet, film or story

- ACQUISITIONS BOARD - the group, typically within a traditional publisher, that determines what books that publisher will acquire

- ADVANCE PRINT RUN - the printing of a quantity of copies undertaken prior to a book's launch date

- AGENT – a person who acts on behalf of another; a literary advocate for authors

- ANTAGONIST – a person who actively opposes someone or something, or gets in the way of someone getting what he/she wants; the person who, if removed from the story, would cause the main conflict to fall apart; the person or thing that forces change in the protagonist

- ARC – short for "Advanced Reader Copy," which publishing houses often submit to reviewers before a book is released

- AUCTION – a public sale in which goods or property are sold to the highest bidder; in a literary auction, an agent often opens the auction for a highly desired manuscript to several interested publishing houses

- AUTHOR – a writer of a book, article or report; someone who writes books as a profession

- BACK COVER BLURB – a short, appealing description of a book written for the back cover

- BACK STORY – a history or background created for a fictional character; usually accounts for events that happened before a story opens and is usually the foundation for a character's Incorrect Core Beliefs, world view or belief system

- BACK STORY DUMP – a passage in a book that interrupts the forward narrative drive of the story by over-explaining what has happened to the character(s) in the past, before the story started

- BEAT – to repeat an element in a scene

- BIG BOOK – often synonymous with a "high concept" book; usually means a book that will appeal to the majority of people and will stand apart from other books on the market in an extremely positive way

- BIG SIX – refers to the six "big" New York publishing houses. They are: Hachette Book Group (Formerly Warner Books, the publisher is known for a few of its larger imprints – Little, Brown & Company and Grand Central); HarperCollins; MacMillan Publishers Ltd (Residing in the New York City's Flatiron building, the MacMillan imprints run the gamut from commercial fiction (St. Martin's Press) through speculative fiction (Tor) and strong literary fiction (Farrar, Straus & Giroux)); Penguin Group   (including the Berkley Division); Random House; Simon & Schuster (including the Pocket imprint).

- BLACK MOMENT - the moment in the story when the hero or heroine's greatest fears with regard to the Internal/Romantic conflict appear to have been realized; this moment is a step backwards wherein the character believes that revealing his true character or being brave enough to change has backfired; it causes the character to temporarily revert back to his/her shell/who they were at the beginning of the story; this black moment precedes the character's greatest realization that will enable him/her to win in the climax

- BLOG/BLOGGING - short for Web Log, a blog is an online journal; blogging is the act of writing or updating one's blog

- BLURB - a short appealing description of a book written for promotional purposes; can occur in an ad, on the book cover, or in a proposal to a publisher

- BOARD MEMBER - a member of a writing chapter, be it on a local or national level, that has volunteered to take on a leadership position in some way

- BOOK DOCTOR - a professional editor who charges money to improve an author's writing

- BRAINSTORM - to generate new ideas (as in, for a story)

- BRAND - a feeling or image that an author develops to associate with his/her name

- BYLAWS - the rules applicable to how an organization is run

- CALL, THE - the moment an agent or author calls to let an author know she is going to represent her or that an offer has been made on the author's work

- CATEGORY - often used to refer to the shorter, serial romances published by Harlequin Enterprises; typically around 50,000 to 70,000 words; are typically part of serial imprints, which each series focused on a particular type of book (sexy, funny, family, suspense, etc)

- CENTRAL STORY QUESTION - asks whether the protagonist will defeat the antagonist and achieve his/her goal. Takes the form of: Will Indy defeat the Nazis and rescue the ark of the covenant?

- CHAPTER - a main division of a book, typically encompassing one or more scenes and usually numbered.

- CHARACTER – a person in a novel, hopefully embodied with both physical and moral qualities, strengths and weaknesses, and a distinctive nature and way of speaking

- CHARACTER ARC – the degree of emotional transformation the protagonist undergoes as a result of the events and conflicts he is forced to face in a story

- CHICK LIT - humorous, sometimes snarky-toned novel that often focuses on young women entering the adult, professional world for the first time. No happy ending is required and the subject matter can be light or weighty. A chick lit mystery usually involves a crime-solving heroine with attitude

- CLIENT – a person using the services of another; generally, a writer is an agent's client, but a writer is not an editor's client, simply the editor's author.

- CLIMAX – the most intense, exciting, or important part of a piece of fiction; a culmination or apex; the moment the protagonist and antagonist in a work of fiction face off in a flight or fight situation

- COMEDY - as in, romantic comedy: romance with a light, humorous tone

- COMMERCIAL FICTION – fiction that is intended to be mass distributed and to make a profit

- CONFLICT – opposition in a work of fiction that motivates plot and character growth

- CONFLICT BOX – a way of analyzing conflict by asking whether what the antagonist is doing to achieve his/her goal is causing the protagonist's conflict (the thing getting in the way of him/her getting his/her goal), and whether what the protagonist is doing to achieve his/her goal is causing the antagonist's conflict (the thing getting in the way of him/her getting his/her goal). According to Jennifer Crusie, if these things are true, an author has created inescapable conflict

- CONTEMPORARY: romance set in the present time where the hero and heroine live in the modern world that most readers can easily relate to

- CONTRACT – a written or spoken agreement that is intended to be enforceable by law

- CO-OP – what a publishing house pays in order to make sure certain books are placed in stores in an advantageous way

- COPY EDITS – editing with the goal of correcting grammar irregularities and inconsistencies and of correcting punctuation, spelling, usage and style

- COVER ART – the artistic images shown on the cover of a book

- CRIT – abbreviation for "critique"

- CRIT GROUP – a group of writers who work together to critique each other's works

- CRIT PARTNER – a person who someone consistently uses to critique her work

- CRITIQUE – to provide a detailed analysis and assessment of another person's story

- CROSSING GENRES – when an author or reader switches between different fiction genres

- DAPHNE – abbreviation for the Daphne du Maurier writing contest put on by the KOD chapter of RWA

- DEBUT – an author's first published work

- DIMINISHING CHOICES – the choices that become more limited to a character as a story progresses

- DOUBT – a feeling of uncertainty or lack of conviction

- EDITOR – a person who is in charge of and determines the final content of a published book

- ELEVATOR PITCH – a very brief, catchy description of one's written work; so called because one should be able to rattle it off to someone he/she meets in an elevator and catch their attention; sometimes used synonymously with log line or high concept pitch

- EPILOGUE – a section at the end of a book that serves as a comment on or conclusion to what has happened

- E-PRESS – a publishing house or press that produces books in digital form

- E-READER – a device for reading books in digital format Example, a Kindle, Sony Reader, or Nook.

- EROTICA – a written work intended to arouse sexual desire; a story in which the sexual journey of the characters is the most important journey

- ESSENCE – a character's true nature when he puts away the mask he hides behind

- EXCLUSIVE – excluding or not admitting other things; to limit someone else's access to a work, as in an agent having an exclusive right to determine whether he or she is going to represent an author—during this time, the author generally agrees not to submit the same work until the agent has made a decision and gotten back to him/her

- EXTERNAL CONFLICT – an external person, thing, or situation that attempts to keep a story's protagonist from achieving his/her goal

- FANTASY – a genre of imaginative fiction involving magic and adventure in a setting other than the real world

- FEEDBACK – comments from others on the quality of one's writing

- FILM RIGHTS – the right of an entity to adapt the work for film
- FIRST SALE – the first time an author is offered and accepts a publishing contract
- FLASHBACK – when a scene diverts from the chronological nature of a story to explore something that happened in a character's past
- FOREIGN RIGHTS – the right of an entity to sell a work of fiction to foreign countries
- FULL – abbreviation for one's complete manuscript
- GALLEY PROOF – a printer's proof of a written work that demonstrates its final form
- GENRE – a category of artistic composition, as in literature characterized by similarities in form, style, or subject matter
- GENRE FICTION – fiction with an expected formula that creates reader expectation
- GOAL – the object of a person's effort or ambition; an aim or desired result
- GMC – abbreviation for goal, motivation, conflict
- GMCD – abbreviation for goal, motivation, conflict, and disaster
- GOLDEN HEART – a writing contest put on annually by RWA for unpublished authors
- HAPPY ENDING – an expected element of a romance novel
- HARLEQUIN LINES – individual imprints of novels that are published by Harlequin Enterprises
- HEAD HOPPING – switching the point of view of your characters within the same scene

- HERO'S JOURNEY – also known as the mythic journey, this technique begins with the hero in his Ordinary World and his reluctance to leave it when he gets the call to adventure. It details the different things and types of people he will encounter once he enters the "new world," completes his journey, and returns back to his Ordinary World with something to share with everyone

- HIGH CONCEPT – a concept for a book or movie that immediately captures the attention and interest of most of the population; According to Alexandra Sokoloff, while a log line can describe an interesting story, she maintains it is not "high concept" unless "everyone who hears it can see exactly what the movie or book is—and a majority of people who hear it will want to see it or read it..." See Chapter 18, *infra*.

- HISTORICAL – a novel set in historical times

- IMPRINT – a brand name under which books are published, sometimes the name of a former publishing house that is now part of a larger group

- INCITING INCIDENT – the thing that causes a protagonist or character to leave his Ordinary World and begin his story journey

- IDENTITY – the mask behind which a character hides his true self

- INCORRECT CORE BELIEF – a principle by which a character lives his life that is incorrect and based on his back story or hard times

- INFO DUMPING – When an author ineffectively tries to provide a reader with critical information in big narrative chunks that slow down the plot or pacing of the story.

- INSECURITY – uncertain, anxious, not confident

- INSPIRATIONAL – a novel based on spiritual inspiration, typically having to do with religious faith and written consistently with the dictates of that faith, usually celebrate traditional Christian values, though they can focus on other faiths

- INTERNAL CONFLICT – a force in opposition that comes from a character's internal thoughts or beliefs that gets in the way of his/her goal

- INTERNATIONAL STANDARD BOOK NUMBER (ISBN) - A unique 13-digit number (10 or 13 digits prior to 2007) that identifies a book to retailers and other interested parties; the barcode on a book

- KISS OF DEATH – RWA's special interest online chapter for mystery and suspense authors

- KOD – abbreviation for Kiss Of Death

- LINE EDITS – editing a published work by line, a line editor critiques a book's voice, tone and phrasing, pacing, character development, accuracy, and focuses on errors in grammar, punctuation and writing style

- LIT SIGNING – An annual event at the RWA National Conference, where authors gather to sign their books. All sales are donated to a charity that supports literacy

- LITERARY FICTION – fiction that is valued for quality of form, not necessarily because of its mass appeal or its ability to make a profit; having a marked style intended to create a particular emotional effect, of which an optimistic view of the world is not one of them; fiction that is designed to be thought-provoking and leave a deeper impression; usually, the language is formal, the imagery is lush and the characters complex

- LOG LINE - a one-sentence description of a film or novel that conveys who the main characters are, what the main conflict is about, and what one can expect with respect to setting and/or mood

- LUCK – a crucial component to getting published
- MARKETING – the action or business of promoting and selling products or services
- MARKETING DEPARTMENT – the department in a publishing house that is in charge of promoting and selling books
- MARKETING PLAN – a document that outlines the specific actions a person plans to take in order to interest potential customers and clients in her product/book and persuade them to buy it
- MASH UP – a combination of seemingly incompatible elements, such as Pride & Prejudice, and Zombies
- MASS MARKET PAPERBACK – a paperback that is produced on a large scale for the masses; a smaller, more economical version of a book often sold in grocery stores and airports
- MCGUFFIN – an object or device in a book that serves merely as a trigger for the plot
- MENTOR – an experienced and trusted advisor
- MIDPOINT – a point somewhere in the middle of a work of fiction in which things have taken a major change or the protagonist commits himself fully to his story journey
- MOTIF – a distinctive feature or dominant idea in a work of fiction
- MOTIVATION – the thing that drives someone to act
- MYSTERY - in a mystery, a crime has already been committed at the beginning and the question is who committed it and why
- MYSTERY (COZY): a cozy mystery is one in which an ordinary person (amateur sleuth) is trying to solve a

crime - There is usually no graphic violence, profanity, or explicit sex

- OFFER - when a publishing house expresses readiness to purchase your written work for consideration subject to your acceptance

- OPENING HOOK - a catchy way the author chooses to get a reader's attention during the first lines of a book.

- PANTSER OR PANTZER - someone who writes "by the seat of her pants," with no or very little outlining done ahead of time

- PARANORMAL - a genre of fiction that involves phenomena or characters beyond normal understanding, but usually set in the real world

- PARTIAL - usually refers to a synopsis and the first three chapters of an author's story

- PEN NAME - a fictional name an author chooses to write under

- PITCH - when a writer describes himself or his work in an attempt to gain representation by an agent, or a book contract by a publisher

- PITCH APPOINTMENT - a scheduled time where an author can describe his or her particular story to an agent or editor

- PLACEMENT - where an author's book is placed in a book store

- PLATFORM - a special skill or background an author has in which to identify herself, relate to others, and gain interest in her written work

- PLOT - the main, external events and action in a story

- PLOT OUT A STORY - to outline the events of one's story before or during the writing of it

- PLOTTING BOARD – a method for plotting one's book by making short notes about ideas for scenes and putting them on a board

- PLOTTING SESSION – a time when writers gather to help each other plot their stories

- PLOTTER – a writer who outlines or plots out his/her scenes or story before he/she starts writing

- POINT OF VIEW – the character through whose eyes a reader is seeing the action of a story

- POV – abbreviation for "Point Of View"

- PREMISE – an assertion or proposition that forms the basis for a fictional work

- PRINT RUN – the number of books printed at one time; usually the first print run is important as it represents your chances of making a name for yourself but it also increases chances that you won't sell enough books so the publisher won't make money

- PROLOGUE – a separate introductory section of a literary work; an event that leads to another event or situation; an event that occurs before the central story begins

- PROMOTION – activity that encourages or supports readers buying an author's books

- PROPOSAL – in publishing, generally an example of an author's work submitted to an agent or editor for consideration; usually consists of a synopsis and the first three chapters of the written work

- PROTAGONIST – the leading character in a work of fiction; the most prominent character; the character that changes and grows the most because of the obstacles he/she encounters in the story

- PUBLICIST – a person responsible for publicizing an author and/or her book

- PUBLISHED – a writer whose written work has been prepared and issued for public sale

- PURPOSE –   a scene must have purpose; if between scenes there is no change in the direction of the plot or in the emotions of your characters, the previous scene has no purpose

- QUERY – in the writing context, when a writer sends an agent or an editor a written inquiry asking whether he/she would be interested in his/her work

- REALIZATION – what a character learns as a result of conflict, adjustment, and reflection; the greatest realization comes right after the black moment so the character can overcome it and win during the climax; this realization is often a restatement of the author's thematic assertion

- RED HERRING – a clue that is intended to be misleading or distracting

- REJECTION – usually, a written refusal by an agent or editor to purchase or take on a writer's written work for representation or publication

- REPRESENTATION – the action of speaking or acting on a writer's professional behalf; what an agent does for a writer

- RESOLUTION – the answer to how a story ends; the answer to a novel's central Story Question

- REVISE – to reconsider or alter a piece of written work

- REVISION LETTER – usually provided by an agent or editor who is interested in a piece of written work but does not want to take it on or purchase it until certain changes are made

- RITA – the annual contest put on by RWA for published authors

- ROMANTICA: as defined by Romance Writers of America's (RWA) special interest chapter, Passionate Ink, erotic romance is about the development of a romantic relationship through sexual interaction. A happily ever after is required as in with any romance, but an erotic romance often has explicit sexual content

- ROYALTIES - payment made to a book's author based on industry standard percentages of sales revenue.

- RWA - abbreviation for Romance Writers of America

- RWR - abbreviation for the Romance Writers Report, the monthly magazine distributed to RWA's members

- SALE - when a writer grants a publisher the rights to a written work in exchange for money

- SAME BUT DIFFERENT - a type of written work that has some of the same components that are currently popular but that is different enough to capture the interest of the general public in a way that other books can't; see also BIG BOOK

- SAVE THE CAT - a term coined by Blake Snyder to mean showing on the page that a character is capable of good deeds

- SCENE - a portion of a written work that is smaller than a chapter and represent a unit of a time or a place where an incident in a story occurs

- SCIENCE FICTION - A novel with imaginary elements that are largely possible within scientific theories. Largely based on writing "rationally" about alternative possibilities, although many elements may require suspending disbelief as well.

- SCHIZOPHRENIA - in general, a mentality or approach characterized by inconsistent or contradictory elements (i.e., writers who vacillate in thinking their writing is great or sucks)

- SECONDARY CHARACTERS – characters who are less important than primary characters, often characters who drive sub plots or secondary plots

- SECONDARY PLOT – a plot that is less important than a main plot; while it might add texture to the main plot, the structure of one is not dependent on the other

- SELF-PUBLISH – when a writer chooses to publish a written work himself/herself rather than with an independent publisher

- SELL THROUGH - refers to the percentage of books shipped that are actually sold; the rest are returned to the publisher

- SEQUEL – a published work that continues the story or develops the Theme of an earlier one; also, a portion of written work that is smaller than a chapter but is different from a scene in that it centers on the mental contemplation of one character

- SEQUENCES – a particular order in which things occur; as in the eight sequences in which movies usually occur; screenwriters use these eight sequences to create movies, and fiction writers can use them to create novels; for more information, see Alexandra Sokoloff's blog, www.thedarksalon.blogspot.com

- SERIES – a number of books coming one after another; a set of books published in a common format or under a common title

- SHADOW – often, a dark area of a character's past that results in that character's Incorrect Core Beliefs

- SINGLE TITLE - a single title book is not published as part of publisher's series category line. It is longer and focuses on more than just the external plot between the hero and heroine.   The novels often have secondary characters and subplots, and the External, Internal, and Romantic Conflicts typically run to the end of the book. Although single titles may be written as a series, each book stands alone in packaging. Single title books are usually around 100,000 words long

- SLUSH PILE - unsolicited manuscripts submitted to publishing houses

- SMALL PRESS - Smaller publishing house that releases books often intended for specialized audiences

- STAKES – one's right to something; something that is at risk

- STATE OF THE MARKET – business analysis of how profitable book sales are for publishers and book sellers; a breakdown of what types of books are selling better than others; a breakdown of how many books or authors publishers are willing to offer contracts to and how much on average they are willing to pay

- STORY – an account of people or events, whether real or not, told for entertainment

- STORY BOARD – a method for outlining or brainstorming the components of an individual story by making notes about what could happen in particular chapters or scenes; a sequence of notes representing plot, dialogue, etc of a book

- STORY QUESTION – asks whether the protagonist will defeat the antagonist in order to get his/her story goal

- SUBMISSION – the act of presenting one's written work to an agent or editor for consideration

- SUBGENRE – a category that fits within a larger category of genre

- SUBPLOT – a subordinate plot in a novel that works concurrently with the main plot and is, in fact, critical to the structure of the main plot

- SUSPENSE - Suspense leads up to a big event or dramatic moment with tension being a primary emotion. This tension is usually one source of the conflict in the story. In a romantic suspense, a crime may have occurred at the beginning, but another crime is going to occur. The main thread it trying to prevent a huge disaster rather than simply who committed a previous one

- SYMBOL – a thing that represents or stands for something else

- SYNOPSIS – a brief summary or outline of the plot of a book, usually submitted to an agent or editor for their consideration

- TAGLINE – a catchphrase or slogan, especially one used in advertising

- TALENT – natural aptitude or skill

- TEN FOR TEN - ten important concepts listed in this book that every writer can benefit from knowing

- THEME – the universal meaning of a novel; an idea that recurs in a work of literature, a prominent or frequently recurring assertion

- THREE ACT STRUCTURE - a type of dramatic structure used for plays, films, and novels; includes beginning, middle, and end; also includes setup (of the location and characters) confrontation (with an obstacle) and resolution (culminating in a Climax)

- THRILLER – a novel with an exciting plot where there is a ticking clock; a story that thrills

- TRACK CHANGES – a tool in a word processing program that highlights changes made to a document

- TRADE PAPERBACK – a book about a particular area of interest published for general consumption; bound with a paper or heavy stock cover, usually with a larger trim size than that of a mass-market paperback

- TURNING POINT – the time in a plot in which a decisive change in a situation/relationship/internal state occurs; major things that happen in story that affects emotion and often escalates the stakes and danger

- TWIST POINT – Mary Buckham and Dianna Love's equivalent of a Turning Point. For more information, see their book, Break Into Fiction®:11 Steps to Building a Story that Sells

- URBAN FANTASY - fantastic elements are incorporated into a modern-day, urban setting. Often protagonists must navigate a fantasy world that coexists with the "real world," and includes elements of magic, or magical/paranormal creatures such as werewolves, fairies, vampires, or witches. Usually, female protagonists struggle to come to terms with their powers and world

- VALIDATION – to demonstrate or prove the value of something

- VANITY PRESS - a publishing house that publishes books at the author's expense

- WIP - abbreviation for "work in progress"

- WOMEN'S FICTION - a story that centers on a woman or primarily women's issues, not necessarily the woman's romantic relationship. Does not necessarily require a happy ending

- WORD - short version of Microsoft Word writing program

- WORLD VIEW – how a character views his/her world

- WRITER – a person who writes books/stories

- YA – abbreviation for "young adult"

- YOUNG ADULT - stories that are written for young adults and project the voice of the young adult from the point of view of a young adult. Deals with Themes that are current and interest the young reader of today, even if the story is set in historical times

4. 100 THINGS EVERY ROMANCE

WRITER SHOULD KNOW OR CONSIDER (Caveat: Some of these suggestions come purely from Virna or Tawny's perspective; again, do what works for you!)

- First thing to do: Become a member of Romance Writers Of America.

- If you have a critique partner that tells you she's a better writer than you – run.

- How to track changes in Microsoft Word.

- What GMCD means.

- When trying to get published, the importance of quality over quantity diminishes slightly; sometimes it's not about writing the best book, but writing about a particular topic before someone else does.

- The typical commission for a literary agent is 15%, but for foreign sales it is 20%.

- Most publishers offer 8% royalty on sales (after the author has earned out his/her advance (i.e., has earned the equivalent of her advance in royalties.)

- A book is considered to have sold well if it sold 50% of its print run.

- The difference between scene and sequel.

- The basics of Three Act Structure.

- Some editors actually like prologues.

- Just because you finally land an agent doesn't mean you'll necessarily sell right away.

- Just because you sell right away doesn't mean you're a better writer than someone who hasn't.

- If a friend tells you that something is "just about business," that's your cue to be on your guard.

- 80% of Americans want to write a book

- Most aspiring writers never finish writing a book.

- 70% of American adults haven't set foot in a bookstore in at least five years.

- 57% of new books are not read to completion.

- 70% of books do not earn back the author's advance, which means they do not make a profit.

- 53% of American readers read fiction: 19% is mystery/suspense; 55% is bought by women.

- 2 million manuscripts are submitted annually with 95% being rejected.

- A fiction book is considered successful if it sells 5,000 copies.

- The average bookstore shopper will spend 8 second looking at a book's front cover, and 15 seconds looking at the back cover.

- Every day, the average American spends 4 hours watching TV, 3 hours listening to the radio, and 14 minutes reading magazines.

- In 2002, the five big NY publishers had sales of $4.102 billion dollars.

- The average first-time author is likely to earn an advance of between 2K and 20K on her first book.

- The six-figure advance for newer or unknown authors is becoming a myth.

- Once a book is sold, it will likely be well over a year before it hits shelves.

- Once you've published a book, it is easier to sell other works in proposal form.

- Don't write to validate your talent—in reality, you'll likely spend more time validating your talent just so you can keep writing.

- If you can revise as you go and still write new stuff, do it; if you get bogged down, stop revising and just keep writing. Revise when the first draft is done.

- Don't start polishing a manuscript until it's complete.

- For every person who hates your book there's probably someone who'll love it.

- Someone who looks unapproachable at a conference could turn out to be a really good friend.

- Someone who gets published didn't take your slot—she just fulfilled the need that your story couldn't. Fulfill the next need.

- Yes, it can take a year for someone to read your work, even if you have an agent.

- Even if you have an agent you may not hear back from all the publishing houses who have your manuscript.

- If you think your agent or editor should have answered your email by now, wait twice as long before you contact them.

- Practice saying, "It takes money to make money, honey."

- Practice saying, "I'll do XXX after I write ten pages."

- Expect family or friends to ask, "So have you gotten published yet?" or "How long are you going to write before you give up?" or "What will you do if you're not published in X years?" Some might mean to be offensive, but most have no idea how hard it is to publish a book or how long it takes.

- Getting published is a great goal so long as you don't use it as a marker for talent.

- Serving on a chapter board not only gives back to the romance writing community, but gets you good exposure.

- Most contest results will be biased, inconsistent, and/or useless. Take what's helpful and don't be surprised or upset by the rest.

- Use contests to target specific final judges for whom you'd like to write.

- Bookstores buy books and then "return" unsold books to the publisher by ripping off the covers, mailing them to the publishing house, and tossing the rest. Hardcover books are "remaindered" and sold for cheap.

- Never piss off the art department, sales department, publicity department or any department at your publisher.

- Most authors do not become friends with their agents or editors.

- The way publishing is run will likely not make any sense to you.

- Some debut authors sell on proposal but few do.

- Most veterans acknowledge that the Rita and the Golden Heart is a crapshoot but you should take your chances anyway.

- If you are nominated for a Rita or Golden Heart, the ceremony is a huge deal; a mini--Oscars event complete with fancy dresses, an emcee, and acceptance speeches.

- It's still a brutal business even after you sell. Can you do it again? Will your numbers be good enough to sell another book?

- What your book run is.

- If you're going to national conference to network, it's best to stay at the hotel the conference is in.

- Most networking is done on the smoker's patio or the bar.

- The person you are pitching to wants you to do well.

- You don't necessarily want a five-book deal.

- It's considered bad manners to slip an agent or editor your ms under a bathroom door stall.

- Some authors consider it rude if you take one of their free books at the RWA book signings without waiting to have them sign it.

- How to use spell check. Also, how to read your manuscript to catch correctly spelled words used in the wrong place (i.e., They're versus their).

- What a proposal consists of.

- How to write a query letter and synopsis.

- Protagonists should have a Character Arc, but antagonists generally should not.

- "All" you have to do is make your characters strong, but not jerks; vulnerable, but not weak; and relatable, but not predictable.

- Don't over use adverbs, tags, or narration.

- Just because an editor loves your writing doesn't mean she can buy your work.

- If you think someone's taking too long to get back to you, they probably haven't even read it yet.

- The only thing you can control is writing the book.

- Group blogs are a lot more fun, and less work, than trying to keep one of your own up-to-date.

- How to Twitter, Facebook, and MySpace.

- What genre you write, what genre is hot, and what genre is going to be hot in the near future.

- Many bestselling authors took years to get an agent or get published. Many of them took years to publish once they got an agent. Many of them almost quit.

- Being "midlist" is not usually thought of as a good thing.

- Harlequin headquarters is based in Canada.

- The difference between alpha and beta.

- How to "save the cat."

- What your brand is.

- You can be a pro even if you haven't submitted a complete ms to an agent or editor, but you can't be an RWA PRO.

- Even if your agent loves you, he/she will likely forward you rejections with a simple "FYI."

- If you need something from your agent or editor, you need to ask for it.

- It's okay to call your agent.

- You only get part of your advance when you sign the contract, the rest comes when you turn in the book and it is accepted, and when the book is actually released.

- Deals reported in Publisher's Weekly may include yet-to-be earned bonuses based on anticipated sales.

- You can always change your pen name.

- Agents are really hard to get. The people who say it's better to have no agent than a bad one might not know your particular situation; on the other hand, this statement has validity. Think long and hard before you make a decision, but then make it and don't look bad.

- An agent who isn't doing things the way you'd do them is not necessarily a bad agent; that said, he/she still might not be the agent for you.

- You can know what "high concept" means and you still might not be able to think of one. On the other hand, if you keep trying, you'll know immediately when you have.

- Workshop presenters at National get part of their conference fee credited; National conference committee chairs and assistants get even more than that waived. But you can only chair a committee once.

- The Dollar Store is a great place to look for promotional materials.

- People don't keep your bookmarks.

- A lot of e-published authors make a great living writing.

- There comes a time you have to stop taking classes and start writing.

- A kind word or act can make the difference between someone finally pursuing their passion or giving it up.

- Your characters can't have sex just to have sex, but because the sex will move the plot forward.

- Eroticas have plots, too.

- If you don't think you'd be turned on by a shape-shifting vampire, you just might be wrong.

- Writing something negative about your agent or editor or another author on the blogosphere can ruin your career, so be careful.

- Think twice about meeting your favorite author; the reality is that some really obnoxious people are great writers — is it worth the risk that you can't ever read her again? More often than not, they're fantastic people.

- When people tell you to take risks, they might not be talking about the kind of risks you end up taking.

- When an agent or editor says your work just wasn't compelling enough, they probably can't even verbalize why your writing didn't grab them—it just didn't.

- Feedback isn't worth a darn thing unless you respect the person who is giving it.

- If you're only writing because you want to strike it rich, buy a lottery ticket.

- Whatever works for you is the secret to writing a good book.

- Comedians take risks at being funny and don't always succeed, the same is going to be true for a writer who wants to tell stories.

- RWA has special interest chapters for those who write mystery, who want to join a chapter on line, who write historicals, etc.

- Never pay an agent or editor to read your work. The money should always be coming to you, not from you. (Okay, so reimbursing for photo copies might be something different.)

- Not all agents have their clients sign contracts. This doesn't necessarily mean they're a "bad" or "questionable" agent.

- There are good agents who don't live in New York.

- Embrace the term "cautiously optimistic."

- The day you quit might be the day you would have sold.

5. THE DETAILS OF VIRNA'S WRITING JOURNEY

September 2006

After years of dreaming about writing a novel, I decided to email a writer who was an acquaintance of a friend of mine. This writer was local and published. I figured I'd simply ask her some questions about the business. She graciously agreed to meet with me.

When I met the writer I'd emailed, I explained that I didn't think I could write within the confines of the "rules" romance required. She looked puzzled and told me there aren't any rules. All you do, she said, is sit down and write the story in your head.

Imagine that.

Later, she invited me to an event by her local chapter of Romance Writers Of America (RWA). It was a reader's luncheon. I sat at her table. I listened to the speaker, a *New York Times* Best Selling Author, tell an inspiring story about persevering despite years of rejection. Eventually, I struck up a conversation with someone sitting across from me. She invited me to join her critique group. Later, at a book signing, I met other writers and saw for myself they were all "ordinary" people, with kids, jobs, and insecurities.

I joined that crit group and connected with the women right away. I felt "at home." I started thinking about my story and began writing regularly, even if it meant writing at two o'clock in the morning.

WHAT I LEARNED:

You don't have to be single, be independently wealthy, or quit your day job to write, nor do you need to have majored in creative writing. To write, all you need is to sit down and write your story. Of course, you need the drive to work hard, the support to logistically do it, and the willingness to ask for help and learn from the experience of others.

October-November 2006

After meeting with my new crit partners several times, I found I thrived with constructive criticism and that I enjoyed giving feedback on other's stories. I'd already written a couple of chapters when my crit partners told me about NaNoWriMo. NaNoWriMo stands for National Novel Writing Month. Every November, writers across the world commit to writing 50,000 new words in the month of November. The main goal is to keep writing forward, not worrying about whether your writing is "good" or not. Encouraged by my crit partners and knowing I wanted to enter RWA's Golden Heart contest, I signed up.

I threw myself into the task of writing 50,000 words on my first manuscript. A few days before the month ended, I had 45,000 words written. What an accomplishment! Plus, I had time to write 5,000 more. Only, I didn't. I looked at where I was and what I'd written and decided I'd done what I'd needed to do. I'd even entered the first 25 pages in a contest, hoping to get additional feedback. Writing more just to finish NaNoWriMo felt like it would be an undue burden based on my other commitments. I understood the importance of being flexible and taking care of all aspects of my life. I set goals, yes, but I also knew I had the power modify them.

WHAT I LEARNED:

To be a writer, you should be driven, but you can also be flexible. Setting a schedule or writing an outline gives you a roadmap, but it doesn't have to lock you in.

November 1-10, 2006

I learned more about what RWA had to offer, including the National Conference, and the opportunity to pitch to editors and agents. I was bummed I'd missed the last conference, which had been in Reno. It had been so close! I began looking into other conferences. One in particular caught my eye. It was billed as a smaller conference (about 60 people) with the chance to pitch to one agent and one editor.

Attending the conference was a major stepping stone for me personally. I hadn't flown in five years because I was afraid to. I rarely traveled and my husband couldn't understand why I'd fly to a writing conference when I didn't have a completed work to pitch. To him, it seemed like a waste of money. However, something inside me wouldn't let it go. By now, I knew that being published was going to be my ultimate goal. So, I signed up for the conference, despite my fear of flying and despite my husband's inability to understand why I needed to.

WHAT I LEARNED: Pursuing writing, as with any creative endeavor, will benefit you in other aspects of your life.

November 11, 2006

I made an appointment to pitch my story to an editor and agent at the conference. While I anxiously waited for my pitch appointment with the editor to start, I chatted with a few other people. One lady offered to help me practice my pitch, which I gladly took her up on. Another woman told me that the attending editor had gladly read someone's pages, which she'd pulled up on her phone, during her pitch appointment. I remembered that I had a synopsis and the first 25 pages of my manuscript in my hotel room (at a different hotel), the same ones I'd entered in my first contest. Although I'd been advised not to bring pages to a pitch, I decided to go back to my hotel room and get them. Just in case.

When I told the editor about my story, she expressed enough interest that I told her I had the pages. She said she wanted to look at them. She scanned the synopsis right there, favorably commenting on one point after another. She then said she'd like to take the first 25 pages with her and read them. My first pitch had gone very well.

The next morning, the editor caught me as I was going into breakfast. She told me she loved the story, that I wrote very well, and that she'd be disappointed if she couldn't acquire the story. She said an offer for the story would likely be in the low five-figure range.

WHAT I LEARNED:

The women in RWA are passionate, talented, supportive, and plain old fun to be around. You can take risks and break the rules, and sometimes it will pay off.

November 13, 2006

So excited I could hardly think straight, I returned home and immediately contacted two agents and queried them about representation. I'd heard one agent speak at a local RWA chapter meeting and had been very impressed with her. (At this point, I'd joined five local RWA chapters.) The second agent was a "hard hitter" and was recommended by one of my crit partners. Unlike the first agent, the second agent didn't seem to have a problem shopping a new author on a partial manuscript rather than a full.

I heard back from both agents right away. Both requested I send them the same synopsis and pages that the editor had read. The first agent, however, wasn't as enthusiastic as I expected her to be. She asked whether I'd had anything published, even e-published, and seemed concerned that I hadn't. In addition, she warned me that the editor's interest didn't amount to a committed offer. After reading my pages, the first agent said the story wasn't right for her. The second agent, however, emailed me to say she liked what she was reading.

WHAT I LEARNED:

Just because you have interest in a book or what seems like an offer, an agent won't necessarily take you on.

November 13-29, 2006 (Over Thanksgiving Break)

I worked on finishing the manuscript to increase my chances of getting an agent and a contract. I finished the manuscript and sent it to the agent.

After receiving and reading the full manuscript, the agent emailed me to tell me she thought it was great. We set up a time to talk on the phone. During that call, she asked if I was amenable to revisions (about 2 pages of notes) because "she wanted to work with me."   I worked on the revisions and sent the revised manuscript back to her, along with a synopsis of my next manuscript. I also told her the good news that my 25 pages had finaled in the contest I'd entered. After one more round of revisions, the agent told me she thought I'd done a great job. She said she'd be able to submit the manuscript in the next week.

WHAT I LEARNED:

Sometimes, in combination with hard work, the stars will align early on.

February 20, 2007

My agent submitted my manuscript to 10 editors at major New York publishing houses.

I received two rejections on my manuscript on March 6, 2007. I received others on March 9, 12, 15, 28, and April 9, 2007. My agent verbally received two more rejections and passed on the news. Every rejection felt like a punch in the gut. Many of them were complimentary, with the editors asking to see future projects. Overall, however, the rejections were vague (as little as "not compelling enough") or inconsistent.

WHAT I LEARNED:

Heartache is a natural part of the business and sometimes waiting to get a rejection is preferable to getting several in a row.

February 20, 2007-June 12, 2007

My agent told me not to worry. I concentrated on completing the second manuscript and brainstormed ideas for the next story.

My agent assured me we would continue to work until I sold. I turned in my second manuscript to my agent and discussed my ideas for the next project. My agent told me that she loved the second manuscript, didn't think anything had to be changed, and that she would submit over the June 4th weekend. When that didn't happen, I nudged my agent, and she apologized, saying she was buried with work. Since we hadn't heard back from the last editor who had the first manuscript (the same editor I'd pitched to), I signed up for a pitch appointment with her at the next National Conference.

WHAT I LEARNED:

You can survive rejection by moving forward and continuing to work on the next project.

July (National RWA Conference) 2007

My agent was still so busy that she hadn't yet had a chance to submit my second manuscript. However, I met with her at the RWA conference in Dallas, TX, and she assured me I was doing everything that I should be. Afterwards, I went to my pitch appointment with the editor I had previously pitched to--the one that had been interested in my book.

When I met with the editor, she sheepishly apologized for not getting back to me and said she was going to have to pass on the manuscript. She felt I'd played it too safe in the end. I was disappointed, but I nonetheless pitched her my second manuscript. She was intrigued by the pitch. I told her I happened to have the synopsis and first 80 pages with me. Since I was her last appointment that day, the editor offered to sit down with me and read my pages. We found some couches and she read the pages and offered me feedback for two hours. She loved what she read. She told me I had proven I could accomplish what I hadn't accomplished in the first manuscript. When I told her I had the full manuscript completed, she told me to send it to her immediately and that she would walk it into her senior editor's office herself.

WHAT I LEARNED:

Despite how good you think you are, you can always improve. Despite setbacks, if you persist and prepare, you will see positive results.

July 17, 2007

I told my agent about my successful pitch appointment. I immediately polished and revised the manuscript (ms2) based on the editor's feedback and then my agent emailed it to her.

A couple of days later, the editor emailed me personally and said she was sorry, that she loved the story and, if it was up to her, she would buy it. Ultimately, however, her senior editor, who made the final decision, hadn't been as enthusiastic. She told me I had real talent and not to give up.

I continued to work on manuscript three (ms3).

WHAT I LEARNED: Even if an editor wants to buy your work, she might not be the editor who makes the decision.

July 2007-January 2008

My agent submitted my second manuscript to 9 editors at major New York publishing houses.

The rejections on the second manuscript came much slower than they did on the first. I concentrated on finishing ms3 and on brainstorming the next story. I ran things by my agent, who was responsive, but getting less so. Sometimes my emails would go unanswered and I began to wonder if "she was still into me." Several months had passed and we had only received 3 rejections out of 9 submissions. My agent told me just to keep moving forward, which I did. I completed my third manuscript and sent it to her. Weeks went by and I didn't hear anything. When I asked her about it, she apologized and said she was behind on her reading.

The more time that passed, the more convinced I became that I wasn't her priority. In fact, I knew this to be true. This agent had several huge authors on her list. Even though I understood they were her priority, I began to wonder if I needed an agent who had more time for me. I asked trusted friends, but everyone told me this was just how the business worked and that I'd be crazy to leave such a wonderful agent. I tended to agree with them. I concentrated on writing the next book.

WHAT I LEARNED: Circumstances and individual needs change. Pay attention to why you're uncomfortable. Try to make small changes before doing something drastic.

January 2008

In the meantime, while I worked on my craft and tried to stay inspired, I came up with an idea for a group blog and asked two friends to join me. We worked on getting our websites up and developing the group blog. I would later learn that an editor who was interested in my work checked out the blog in order to find out more about me.

WHAT I LEARNED: Sometimes, combining strengths with others will get you through difficult times. It's never too early to prepare to be published

April 2008

It had been 12 weeks since I'd given my agent my third manuscript but I hadn't heard from her yet. After much agonizing, I emailed my agent and told her I was honored to have been her client, but that I thought she was too busy for me. I asked if she would mind recommending me to a more junior agent.

After I sent my email, the agent's assistant emailed me back. She said my agent was out of town, but that she'd gotten my email and wanted to recommend another agent. I emailed this agent, who happened to be my friend's agent and was someone I was very interested in, and emailed her my third manuscript. My former agent later emailed me personally and said she was sorry things hadn't worked out between us. She conceded she was extremely busy. She gave me referrals to two other agents, invited me to the agency's party at National, and said to let her know if I ever needed anything.

WHAT I LEARNED: A situation that another person envies still might not be the right situation for you. You can get advice from others, but ultimately you have to trust your instincts, even if everyone else thinks you're crazy (and sometimes you do, too). Always try to act with integrity and respect. It's a small business and you need every friend you can get.

September 2008

While I waited for my targeted agent (Agent2) to read my third manuscript, I sent a proposal of my first manuscript to a category line at Harlequin. Subsequently, I nudged Agent2, who said she was terribly behind. She asked for my patience because she really wanted to finish reading my manuscript.

Even though I didn't have an agent, I sent proposals of my manuscripts to two editors I met at the RWA National Conference. Both requested full manuscripts. I also sent some queries to a few other agents, just in case Agent2 passed. One agent asked for a full manuscript. Some passed. Agent2 emailed and said she had some major structural revisions for the next manuscript and it was up to me whether I wanted to do them. Of course, I did. Luckily, I'd already anticipated most of changes based on feedback I was receiving from the editors and agents I'd recently queried. As such, it didn't take me long to make the revisions Agent2 wanted. I sent Agent2 the revised manuscript. Agent2 offered to represent me on December 4, 2008, while I was on a family vacation in Disney World. Happy day!

WHAT I LEARNED: Don't rest on your laurels. There's always something you can do to benefit your career.

January-April 2009

Having worked on a new manuscript for the category line I was targeting, I sent Agent2 the full manuscript. Agent2 submitted my already-completed third manuscript to 8 editors at major New York publishing houses. The rejections started coming in, one by one.

To distract myself, I decided to try my hand at a completely different kind of story. As Agent2 was nudging editors for responses on manuscript three, she submitted the full manuscript of the category story I had sent her. Then, I sent her the full on my next project. My agent read the beginning on the flight to a conference we were both attending. When I saw her, she said she'd loved it. She said when I had proposed writing a sexy contemporary without any suspense, she wasn't sure I could pull it off, but that I had.

WHAT I LEARNED: Being well-read opens you up to other possibilities. Constantly assess different ways to get what you want because you may find you have talents for other things.

April 2009

I sat down with Agent2 at the conference to discuss what my next step should be. She said she didn't understand why manuscript three had been rejected because it was good, but that it was probably a result of the market and the downturn in the economy. She said it was getting harder to sell and that I should really try to make my next project a BIG book that was part of a series. After returning home, I began brainstorming big or high concept ideas. In particular, I concentrated on what I loved to write (suspense) and what several agents at the conference had said the market was looking for — paranormal.

I wrote up about five different ideas and sent them to my agent for her feedback. One idea had me particularly excited, because it didn't seem like something that had been done before, at least not the way I envisioned it. I began writing a proposal for the idea and found that I absolutely loved writing paranormal suspense — a genre I enthusiastically read but never thought I'd write.

WHAT I LEARNED: Listen to those who have more experience than you, then do something meaningful with their advice. Be willing to try new things.

April 21, 2009

I finished the proposal for my big series idea and sent it to my agent. She read the proposal and said she loved it, and that she'd called around. Editors were excited about the idea. With her feedback, I polished the proposal and sent it back to her. She then submitted the proposal to several editors.

The next day, I received an email from my agent. She said that one editor (Editor2--an editor who'd read my third manuscript and liked my writing) had read the newest proposal overnight and LOVED it.

WHAT I LEARNED: Sometimes if it feels high concept, it is high concept.

April 30-May 30, 2009

We received some rejections on the newest proposal. However, it was clear from the feedback that the editors were more excited about this story than any of the ones I'd written thus far. Editor2 got a strong second read and was enthusiastic about the story, but confirmed she couldn't buy anything without having the full manuscript in hand. She said she would give me revision notes if I was amenable to seeing them. Of course, I was.

I wrote the rest of the manuscript and incorporated the revisions that Editor2 wanted. I wrote the full quickly. Likewise, my agent revised quickly. We both knew we had hit something special and we didn't want to lose momentum or take the chance that someone else would submit a similar story before I finished mine. Within three weeks, my agent sent Editor2 a polished full manuscript.

WHAT I LEARNED: Sometimes, you need to put everything else aside and concentrate solely on what you need to do.

June 1-15, 2009

We soon heard that Editor2 loved the full manuscript and had put it out for second reads. While we waited, I learned that one of my fellow bloggers was attending a conference put on by one of my favorite authors. I'd wanted to go, but it was the same weekend as my local chapter retreat.

At the conference, my fellow blogger pitched to an editor and handed her a business card with the URL for our group blog. It turns out, it was Editor2. Editor2 looked at the card, smiled, and said, "I know Virna De Paul. I love that blog."

WHAT I LEARNED: People read your blogs and will know who you are, so be professional and respectful.

June 16-24, 2009

Editor2 contacted my agent and told her she had full editorial support for my manuscript. In other words, all the editors loved it and she couldn't be in a better position to bring it in front of the publishing house's acquisitions committee.

Despite the editor's love for the series, the publishing house's marketing department had concerns about bringing on another debut paranormal author. They were already launching three new authors and were afraid bringing in another would detract from the others.

WHAT I LEARNED: You can have talent, connections, and an editor who loves your book and wants to buy it and still not sell. Bottom line: you need luck to sell a novel.

June 24, 2009

My agent forwarded me a great note from Editor2. She said she was so disappointed not to have been able to buy my book.

Editor2 said she was sure I'd sell to another house and she offered to give me the revision notes she'd made on the full manuscript. I gratefully (albeit, tearfully) accepted and used those notes to make the manuscript even stronger. My agent assured me she believed in me and gave me permission to throw a pity party for the night—then she said tomorrow I should get back to work.

WHAT I LEARNED: There are kind people who want to help you even if they won't get anything out of it.

June-July 2009

I grieved. The next day, I brainstormed more ideas and started to write a marketing plan that would help publishers see how I could stand apart from other writers.

I submitted the plan to my agent. Even though I wasn't registered for the RWA National Conference in Washington D.C. and couldn't afford to register, I decided to stay at the hotel during the conference and meet with Editor2 and another editor whose read of a proposal I'd bought on Brenda Novak's online auction for diabetes. I was able to talk to Editor2 about what other types of projects she was looking for. I also got feedback from the other editor on my proposal and she offered to look at it again after I made revisions.

WHAT I LEARNED: When all seems lost, remind yourself and others why you're so special. Keep trying to make connections. Life goes on, and so will you.

July 23, 2009

After I revised the full manuscript of the paranormal that had been rejected by the marketing department of one house, I sent it to my agent. My agent then submitted that full manuscript to two additional editors.

While I waited, I decided to work on another series based on what I'd learned at conference. I wrote a proposal for a new manuscript that I was excited about. In the meantime, I learned that an editor who had the full paranormal (Editor3) had loved it and was getting a second read.

WHAT I LEARNED: There's always a new story in me.

August–November 2009

My agent submitted the new proposal to Editor2. Although she thought it was very well written, Editor2 said it wasn't what they were looking for at the time. I brainstormed another idea, this one another paranormal. I wrote up a proposal.

My agent loved the new paranormal proposal and sent it to Editor2. Although Editor2 didn't love it as much as she'd loved my previous paranormal series, it prompted her to talk to another editor who'd loved my work, as well. This editor was the head of a category line and indicated she'd be very interested in establishing the first paranormal series (the one that marketing had shot down) for that line. She asked my agent if I was willing to trim a single title into a category book.

WHAT I LEARNED: Hard work doesn't always glean the results you want, but it will pay off somehow; if you persevere, people will remember you and take you seriously.

November 16-18, 2009

Because I had no problem starting my career in category and building a readership, and because I loved the paranormal series so much and knew the editors who were interested would do it justice, I shortened the manuscript from 104,000 words to 76,000 words. I sent the manuscript to my agent. Then, I decided, I was ready for a break.

On November 18, 2009, Agent2 called me and said Editor3 had made an offer on the single title version of the paranormal series. The call came when I was least expecting it. I was thrilled. Beyond thrilled. However, as excited as I was, it didn't feel real. It wouldn't truly sink in for several weeks. By then, I needed to begin working on the next book.

WHAT I LEARNED: Sometimes it's about the last man standing. Or, in this case, the last writer standing. Even as you celebrate one accomplishment, keep your eye on the next challenge ahead.

RECOMMENDED SOURCES

(Note: this list is not exhaustive nor is the absence of a title or organization meant to imply it is not a worthy source.)

<u>Organizations & Websites</u>:
Mystery Writers of America - http://mysterywriters.org
Novelists, Inc - http://www.ninc.com
Romance Writers of America - http://www.rwanational.org
Science Fiction & Fantasy Writers of America - http://www.sfwa.org
Sisters in Crime - http://sistersincrime.org
eHarlequin - http://www.eharlequin.com
www.lovewritingbook.com

<u>Writing Books</u>:
Plot & Structure – James Scott Bell
Scene & Structure – Jack Bickham
The 38 Most Common Fiction Writing Mistakes – Jack Bickham
Break Into Fiction – Mary Buckham and Dianna Love
Self Editing for Fiction Writers – Browne & King
The Artist's Way – Julia Cameron
Getting the Words Right: How to rewrite, edit and revise – T. A. Rees Cheney
Writing Dialogue – Tom Chiarella
Heroes & Heroines – Cowden, LaFever & Viders
Plot – Ansen Dibell
GMC: Goal, Motivation & Conflict – Deb Dixon
Finding your Voice – Les Edgerton
Creating Character Emotions – Ann Hood
Building Better Plots – Robert Kernen
On Writing – Steven King
The Newbie's Guide To Publishing – J.A. Konrath

Beginnings, Middles & Ends – Nancy Kress
Writing the Breakout Novel – Donald Maas
The Fire in Fiction – Donald Maas
Coaching the Artist Within – Eric Maise
The Novel Writer's Toolkit – Bob Mayer
Story – Robert McKee
Writing the Romantic Comedy – Billy Mernit
Conflict, Action & Suspense – William Noble
Novelists Essential Guide to Crafting Scenes – Raymond Obstfeld
The War of Art – Steven Pressfield
How to Tell a Story: The Secrets of Writing Captivating Tales – Rubie and
Provost
45 Master Characters – Victoria Schmidt
Screenwriting Tricks For Author (And Screenwriters) – Alexandra Sokoloff
Creating Characters: How to Build Story People – Dwight Swain
Techniques of the Selling Writer – Dwight Swain
Theme & Strategy – Ronald Tobias
The Comic Toolbox – John Vorhaus
Got High Concept? – Lori Wilde

<u>Motivational Books</u>:
The Secret – Rhonda Byrne
The Success Principles – Jack Canfield
The Seven Principles of Success – Stephen Covey
The Seven Spiritual Laws of Success – Deepak Chopra
Excuses Begone – Wayne Dyer
Real Magic – Wayne Dyer
You'll See It When You Believe It – Wayne Dyer
Awaken the Giant Within – Tony Robbins
Unlimited Power – Tony Robbins
The Key – Joe Vitale

Made in the USA
Lexington, KY
14 January 2013